Programming Power

Essential Skills for a Successful Career in Tech

Efren Cronin

Foreword

Welcome to the world of programming! Whether you're a curious beginner embarking on your coding journey or an experienced developer looking to expand your knowledge, this book is your gateway to the exciting realm of software development.

In these pages, you will find a comprehensive and approachable guide that covers the essential concepts and skills needed to become a proficient programmer. From the fundamentals of programming and understanding different programming languages to mastering data structures, algorithms, and object-oriented programming, this book offers a solid foundation for your coding endeavors.

But why learn programming? The answer lies in the endless possibilities and opportunities it presents. Programming empowers you to bring ideas to life, solve problems, and create innovative solutions. It allows you to unleash your creativity and opens doors to a multitude of industries, from web development and mobile app creation to data science and machine learning.

Throughout this book, you will explore various programming languages, including Python, JavaScript, Java, C++, and more. You will gain insights into the syntax, data types, control flow, functions, and error handling techniques specific to each language. With hands-on examples, you'll build a strong understanding of these languages and their application in real-world scenarios.

But programming is more than just writing code. It's about problem-solving, logical thinking, and continuous learning. This book will guide you through the process of analyzing problems, designing algorithms, and debugging your code. You'll also discover the importance of testing, refining, and documenting your projects, ensuring they meet high standards of quality and reliability.

Whether you're interested in web development, data analysis, or mobile app creation, this book covers a wide range of topics that will equip you with the skills to tackle exciting projects. You'll delve into web technologies like HTML, CSS, and JavaScript, gaining the ability to build simple web applications. You'll also explore the foundations of data science, learning how to manipulate and visualize data using Python.

One of the remarkable aspects of programming is its collaborative nature. With the knowledge and skills you'll acquire, you'll be able to contribute to open-source projects, collaborate with other developers, and learn from a vast community of coding enthusiasts.

So, take a deep breath, embrace the challenge, and dive into the chapters that lie ahead. Let this book be your trusted companion as you embark on your programming journey. Remember, programming is both an art and a science, and it rewards those who are persistent, curious, and passionate.

Happy coding!

Summary

Foreword 3

Chapter 1: Introduction to Programming 23

What is Programming? 23

Problem Solving 24

Programming Languages 24

Syntax 25

Variables and Data Types 25

Control Structures 25

Functions 25

Algorithms 26

Debugging..26

Testing 26

Software Development Life Cycle 26

Continuous Learning 26

Why Learn Programming?..28

Common Programming Languages 32

Python..32

JavaScript..32

Java..32

C++: 33

C#:..33

Ruby..33

PHP 33

Swift 34

TypeScript..34

Go..34

R..34

MATLAB 34

Rust..35

Kotlin 35

Swift 35

SQL 36

Perl 36

Shell scripting 36

Scala 36

HTML/CSS 37

Setting Up Your Development Environment 38

Choose an Operating System 38

Install a Text Editor or Integrated Development Environment (IDE): 38

Install the Programming Language(s) 39

Set Up a Command-Line Interface (CLI): 39

Install Version Control Software 39

Install Additional Tools and Libraries 39

Configure your Environment 40

Test Your Environment 40

Chapter 2: Fundamentals of Programming 42

Variables and Data Types 42

Variables: 42

Data Types: 43

Numeric Types: 43

Boolean: 43

Array/List: 44

Dictionary/Map 44

Tuple 44

Custom/User-Defined Types 44

Integer 45

Floating-Point 45

String 45

Boolean 45

Array/List 46

Dictionary/Map 46

Tuple 46

Operators and Expressions 48

  Operators: 48

  Arithmetic Operators: 48

  Assignment Operators: 49

  Comparison Operators: 49

  Logical Operators: 49

  Bitwise Operators: 50

  Expressions: 50

  String Concatenation: 52

  Increment and Decrement Operators: 52

  Compound Assignment Operators: 53

  Operator Precedence and Associativity: 53

  Ternary Operator: 54

  Operator Overloading: 54

Control Flow: Conditionals and Loops 56

  Conditionals: 56

  If Statement: 56

  If-Else Statement: 57

  If-Elif-Else Statement: 57

  Loops: 58

  While Loop: 58

  For Loop: 58

  Nested Loops: 59

  Loop Control Statements: 59

Functions and Modularization 60

  Functions: 60

  Function Declaration: 60

  Return Statement: 61

  Parameters and Arguments: 62

  Modularization: 62

  Reusability: 62

  Code Organization and Readability: 63

Abstraction and Encapsulation: 63

Collaboration and Collaboration: 63

Testing and Debugging: 64

Chapter 3: Getting Started with a Language (e.g., Python) 65

Installing Python 65

Running Your First Program 68

Open a text editor: 68

Write your Python code 68

Save your program 69

Open a command prompt or terminal 69

Navigate to the program's directory 69

Run your Python program 69

Observe the output 70

Input and Output 72

Input: 72

Reading from the Keyboard: 72

Command-Line Arguments: 73

File Input: 73

Output: 73

Printing to the Console: 74

Writing to Files: 74

Displaying Graphics or User Interfaces: 74

Variables and Data Types in Python 76

Variables: 76

Data Types: 77

Numeric Types: 77

String (str): 77

Boolean (bool): 77

List (list): 78

Tuple (tuple): 78

Dictionary (dict): 78

Set (set): 78

Type Conversion:...79

Expressions in Python.. 80

Control Flow in Python 82

Conditional Statements (if, elif, else): 82

Loops: 83

Exception Handling (try, except, finally): 84

Chapter 4: Working with Data Structures..86

Arrays and Lists...86

Lists: 86

Arrays: 87

Strings 90

Creating Strings: 90

String Manipulation:... 90

String Indexing and Slicing: 91

String Methods:...92

String Concatenation: 92

String Formatting: 92

String Immutability: 93

Dictionaries and Sets 94

Dictionaries: 94

Sets:...95

Tuples 98

Creating Tuples: 98

Immutable: 99

Ordered and Indexing: 99

Heterogeneous Elements: 99

Multiple Assignment and Unpacking:..100

Use Cases:...100

Working with Data Structures in Python 102

Lists: 102

Tuples: 102

Dictionaries: 103

Sets: 103

Arrays: 103

Strings: 104

Chapter 5: Object-Oriented Programming (OOP) Basics 105

Introduction to OOP 105

Objects: 105

Classes: 105

Encapsulation: 106

Inheritance: 106

Polymorphism: 106

Abstraction: 107

Modularity: 107

Classes and Objects 109

Classes: 109

Objects: 110

Inheritance and Polymorphism 113

Inheritance: 113

Polymorphism: 115

Encapsulation and Abstraction 118

Encapsulation: 118

Abstraction: 120

OOP in Python 123

Defining Classes: 123

Creating Objects: 124

Inheritance: 125

Polymorphism: 126

Chapter 6: Error Handling and Debugging 129

Common Types of Errors 129

Syntax Errors: 129

Runtime Errors (Exceptions): 129

Logical Errors: 130

Name Errors: 130

Type Errors:...130

Attribute Errors:...131

Debugging Techniques and Tools..132

Print Statements:...132

Debugging Statements:..132

Logging:..133

IDE Debugging Tools:...133

Error Messages and Stack Traces:..133

Unit Testing:...134

Code Inspection and Review:...134

Debugging Tools and Libraries:..134

Breakpoints:...134

Conditional Breakpoints:..135

Debugging Profilers:...135

Remote Debugging:..135

Documentation and Online Resources:..136

Rubber Duck Debugging:..136

Collaborative Debugging:..136

Exception Handling in Python..138

try-except Block:...138

Multiple Except Blocks:..139

Handling Multiple Exceptions in a Single Except Block:......................140

Optional else Block:...141

finally Block:...142

Raising Exceptions:..143

Best Practices for Debugging...145

Understand the Expected Behavior:..145

Reproduce the Issue:..145

Use Version Control:...146

Analyze Error Messages and Logs:..146

Use Debugging Tools:...146

Debugging Techniques:...147

Write Unit Tests:...147

Collaborate and Seek Assistance:...147

Document the Bug and Fix:...148

Test with Minimal Code: 148

Check Assumptions: 148

Step Through the Code:...149

Debug in Different Environments: 149

Read the Documentation: 149

Use Code Reviews:...150

Take Breaks:..150

Learn from Debugging: 150

Chapter 7: File Handling and Input/Output Operations 152

Reading and Writing Text Files..152

Reading from a Text File: 152

Read the File Contents: 152

Close the File:...153

Writing to a Text File:..154

Write to the File:..154

Close the File:...155

Working with CSV and JSON Files 157

Working with CSV Files:..157

Working with JSON Files: 159

Writing JSON Files:..160

File Manipulation in Python 162

Opening and Closing Files:..162

Reading File Contents: 163

Writing to Files: 164

File Management and Metadata: 165

Standard Input and Output..167

Standard Input (stdin): 167

Standard Output (stdout):...168

Formatting Output: 168

Redirecting Output: 170

Chapter 8: Introduction to Algorithms and Problem Solving 171

What is an Algorithm? 171

Well-defined: 171

Finite: 171

Input and Output: 172

Deterministic: 172

Efficiency: 172

Modularity: 172

Analysis: 173

Problem-solving Paradigms: 173

Optimization: 173

Algorithmic Complexity Classes 174

Algorithm Design Patterns 174

Algorithm Libraries and Resources 174

Understanding Problem Solving Approaches 176

Understand the Problem: 176

Define the Problem: 176

Gather Information: 176

Analyze the Problem: 177

Generate Potential Solutions: 177

Evaluate and Select the Best Solution: 177

Develop an Action Plan: 178

Implement the Solution: 178

Test and Evaluate the Solution: 178

Iterate and Refine: 178

Document and Communicate: 179

Learn from Experience: 179

Common Algorithms and Data Structures 180

Algorithms: 180

Data Structures: 182

Algorithm Design Techniques 185

Divide and Conquer:.. 185

Greedy Algorithms:.. 185

Dynamic Programming:.. 186

Backtracking: 186

Brute Force: 187

Randomized Algorithms: 187

Heuristic Algorithms: 187

Branch and Bound: 188

Reduction:... 188

Approximation Algorithms: 189

Randomized Algorithms: 189

Parallel and Distributed Algorithms:................................... 189

Online Algorithms: 190

Metaheuristic Algorithms: 190

Chapter 9: Introduction to Web Development.......................... 192

Basics of HTML.. 192

HTML Document Structure: 192

HTML Tags and Elements: 193

Common HTML Elements: 193

Attributes: 194

Nesting and Hierarchical Structure:.................................... 194

Semantic HTML: 194

CSS Fundamentals.. 196

CSS Syntax: 196

CSS Selectors: 196

CSS Properties and Values: 197

CSS Cascading and Specificity: 198

CSS Inheritance: 198

CSS Media Queries: 199

CSS Box Layout and Flexbox:.. 199

JavaScript Essentials 200

Variables and Data Types:...200

Operators and Expressions:..200

Control Flow:..201

Functions:..201

Objects:..201

Arrays:..202

DOM Manipulation:...202

Events:..202

Error Handling:..203

Asynchronous Programming:..203

Libraries and Frameworks:..203

Building Simple Web Applications..205

Plan and Design:..205

Set up the Project:...205

Structure the HTML:...205

Style with CSS:..206

Add Interactivity with JavaScript:...206

Test and Debug:...207

Deploy:...207

Iterate and Refine:..207

Chapter 10: Version Control with Git..209

Introduction to Version Control...209

Install Git:...209

Initialize a Repository:...209

Track Changes:..210

Commit Changes:..210

View History:...210

Branching and Merging:...211

Collaborate with Remote Repositories:...211

Resolving Conflicts:..212

Setting Up Git...213

Download and Install Git:...213

Configure Git:..213

Check Git Version: 214

Optional Configuration: 214

Generate SSH Key (Optional): 214

Basic Git Commands 216

git init: 216

git status: 216

git commit -m "Commit message": 217

git push: 217

git pull: 217

git branch: 218

git checkout <branch-name>: 218

git merge <branch-name>: 218

git log: 219

Collaborating with Others Using Git 220

Forking a Repository: 220

Cloning a Repository: 220

Adding an Upstream Remote: 221

Creating and Switching Branches: 221

Making and Committing Changes: 221

Pushing Changes to Your Forked Repository: 222

Creating a Pull Request: 222

Syncing with Upstream Changes: 223

Chapter 11: Testing and Debugging Your Code 224

Importance of Testing 224

Detecting and Preventing Bugs: 224

Ensuring Software Functionality: 224

Improving Software Quality: 225

Enhancing User Confidence: 225

Validating System Performance: 225

Supporting Maintenance and Upgrades: 226

Ensuring Compatibility: 226

Reducing Development Costs: 226

Regulatory and Compliance Requirements: 227

Continuous Improvement: 227

Types of Testing 228

Unit Testing: 228

Integration Testing: 228

System Testing: 229

Acceptance Testing: 229

Performance Testing: 229

Security Testing: 230

Regression Testing: 230

Usability Testing: 231

Exploratory Testing: 231

Continuous Integration and Continuous Testing: 231

Writing Test Cases..233

Identify Test Scenarios: 233

Define Test Objectives: 233

Write Clear and Concise Test Case Titles:..234

Specify Preconditions: 234

Describe Test Steps:..234

Include Expected Results: 234

Add Additional Details and Data:..235

Consider Positive and Negative Scenarios:...235

Make Test Cases Independent and Reusable:.......................................235

Review and Validate Test Cases: 236

Maintain Test Case Documentation:...236

Debugging Techniques and Tools..237

Print Statements: 237

Debuggers:...237

Breakpoints: 238

Logging: 238

Error Messages and Stack Traces:...239

Code Review and Pair Programming: 239

Automated Testing: 239

Online Communities and Forums: 240

Chapter 12: Introduction to Data Science and Analysis.................241

What is Data Science? 241

Data Collection and Storage:...241

Data Cleaning and Preprocessing: 242

Exploratory Data Analysis (EDA): 242

Machine Learning:...242

Statistical Analysis:...243

Data Visualization:..243

Big Data Technologies: 243

Domain Knowledge: 244

Data Manipulation with Python..245

NumPy: 245

Pandas:...245

Data Cleaning: 246

Data Transformation:..246

Filtering and Querying: 246

Merging and Joining Data:..247

Reshaping and Pivot Tables:...247

Handling Dates and Time Series: 247

Data Visualization Basics 249

Choosing the Right Chart Type:..249

Visual Encodings: 249

Labels and Titles:...250

Color Choice:..250

Data Scaling and Axis Limits: 251

Annotations and Highlights:..251

Simplification and Emphasis: 251

Iterative Design and Feedback:...252

Introduction to Machine Learning...253

Data:...253

Training Data and Labels: 254

Algorithms and Models: 254

Training and Evaluation: 255

Feature Engineering: 255

Prediction and Inference: 256

Unsupervised Learning: 256

Deployment and Iterative Improvement: 256

Chapter 13: Introduction to Mobile App Development 258

Mobile App Development Platforms 258

Android Studio: 258

Xcode: 259

React Native: 259

Flutter: 260

Xamarin: 260

PhoneGap/Cordova: 261

Appcelerator Titanium: 261

Native vs. Cross-Platform Development 263

Native Development: 263

Cross-Platform Development: 264

Factors to Consider: 265

Building a Simple Mobile App 267

Define the App Idea: 267

Plan the App Structure and Flow: 267

Choose the Development Approach: 267

Set Up the Development Environment: 268

Develop the App's UI and Features: 268

Test and Debug: 269

Refine the App's Design: 269

Perform User Acceptance Testing: 269

Prepare for Deployment: 270

Deploy and Publish: 270

Monitor, Update, and Maintain: 270

Chapter 14: Final Project and Beyond 271

Selecting a Project Idea 271

Identify a Problem or Need: 271

Research Market Demand: 271

Define Your Target Audience: 272

Evaluate Feasibility and Complexity: 272

Brainstorm and Refine Ideas: 272

Consider Monetization Potential: 273

Validate the Idea: 273

Assess Technical Requirements: 273

Align with Your Interests and Expertise: 273

Balance Innovation and Execution: 274

Planning and Designing Your Project 275

Define Project Goals and Objectives: 275

Identify Target Audience: 275

Create User Personas: 276

Conduct Market Research: 276

Outline App Features and Functionality: 276

Design User Interface (UI) and User Experience (UX): 277

Develop a Technical Architecture: 277

Plan Iterative Development: 277

Create a Project Timeline: 278

Consider Security and Privacy: 278

Test and QA Strategy: 278

Define Metrics and Analytics: 278

Establish a Budget: 279

Collaboration and Communication: 279

Implementing Your Project 280

Set Up the Development Environment: 280

Break Down the Project into Tasks: 280

Start with the Core Functionality: 281

Follow Coding Best Practices: 281

Implement User Interface (UI) and User Experience (UX): 281

Integrate Backend Services: 282

Test and Debug: 282

Optimize Performance: 283

Implement Error Handling and Exceptional Cases: 283

Incorporate Analytics and Tracking: 283

Regularly Review and Refactor Code: 284

Documentation: 284

Version Control and Collaboration: 284

Iterative Development: 285

Prepare for Deployment: 285

Testing and Refining Your Project 286

Test Plan Creation: 286

Functional Testing: 286

Usability Testing: 287

Performance Testing: 287

Compatibility Testing: 287

Security Testing: 288

Error Handling and Exception Testing: 288

Beta Testing: 288

Continuous Integration and Regression Testing: 289

Analyze User Feedback and Metrics: 289

Iterative Refinement: 289

Documentation and Knowledge Sharing: 290

Conclusion 291

Chapter 1: Introduction to Programming

What is Programming?

Programming is the process of creating a set of instructions or code that a computer can understand and execute. It involves writing, testing, and maintaining sequences of instructions in a programming language to solve specific problems or perform desired tasks.

At its core, programming is about problem-solving and providing step-by-step instructions for a computer to follow. These instructions are written using a specific programming language, which serves as a communication medium between humans and computers.

Programs can range from simple scripts that automate repetitive tasks to complex software applications that power various technologies we use every day. Programming enables the development of websites, mobile apps, video games, artificial intelligence systems, data analysis tools, and much more.

To write a program, programmers need to understand the logic and concepts of programming, including variables, data types, control structures (like loops and conditionals), functions, and algorithms. They also need to be familiar with the syntax and rules of the programming language they are using.

Programming allows individuals to leverage the power of computers to automate tasks, process data, and solve problems more efficiently. It requires logical thinking, attention to detail, creativity, and continuous learning, as the field of programming is constantly evolving with new technologies and programming languages being developed.

Programming involves several key concepts and processes:

Problem Solving: Programming is essentially a problem-solving activity. It requires breaking down complex problems into smaller, more manageable tasks and devising algorithms or step-by-step procedures to solve them.

Programming Languages: Programming languages are used to write instructions that computers can understand. Examples of popular programming languages include Python, Java, C++,

JavaScript, and Ruby. Each language has its syntax, rules, and specific use cases.

Syntax: Programming languages have specific syntax, which refers to the rules and structure that govern how instructions are written. Syntax errors occur when the code does not adhere to the language's rules.

Variables and Data Types: Variables are used to store and manipulate data within a program. Data types define the nature of the data stored in variables, such as integers, floating-point numbers, strings, booleans, and more.

Control Structures: Control structures determine the flow of a program's execution. Common control structures include conditional statements (if-else, switch), loops (for, while), and branching (break, continue).

Functions: Functions are reusable blocks of code that perform specific tasks. They allow for modularization and code reuse, improving code organization and readability.

Algorithms: Algorithms are step-by-step procedures or recipes for solving a specific problem. They provide a logical sequence of instructions to solve a problem efficiently. Understanding algorithms is crucial for developing efficient and optimized programs.

Debugging: Debugging is the process of finding and fixing errors or bugs in a program. It involves identifying and resolving issues that prevent the program from running correctly or producing the expected results.

Testing: Testing is the process of evaluating a program's functionality and correctness. It involves running the program with different inputs to ensure it behaves as expected and produces the desired output.

Software Development Life Cycle: Programming is often part of a broader software development life cycle, which includes steps such as requirements gathering, design, coding, testing, deployment, and maintenance.

Continuous Learning: Programming is a field that requires continuous learning and keeping up with advancements.

Technologies, programming languages, and best practices evolve rapidly, and programmers need to stay updated to improve their skills and stay relevant.

By understanding these fundamental concepts and processes, beginners can lay a solid foundation for learning and mastering programming. With practice and hands-on experience, they can develop the skills to create their own programs and solve a wide range of real-world problems.

Why Learn Programming?

Learning programming offers numerous benefits and opportunities in today's technology-driven world. Here's a continuous and easy-to-read explanation of why learning programming is valuable:

In the digital age we live in, programming has become an increasingly essential skill. Whether you aspire to be a software developer, work in data analysis, or simply want to gain a deeper understanding of how technology functions, learning programming opens up a world of possibilities.

One of the primary reasons to learn programming is the ability to create. Programming empowers you to transform your ideas into tangible products. Whether it's a website, a mobile app, or even a game, programming allows you to bring your creative visions to life. You gain the ability to shape technology according to your needs and preferences, enabling you to build something unique and valuable.

Moreover, programming provides you with problem-solving skills that are highly sought after in today's job market. The process of writing code involves breaking down complex problems into smaller, more manageable pieces, and developing logical solutions. These problem-solving abilities extend beyond the realm of technology and can be applied to various aspects of life, making you a more adaptable and effective thinker.

Learning programming also enhances your analytical skills. You learn to think critically, identify patterns, and develop algorithms to solve problems efficiently. Programming encourages a structured and logical approach to finding solutions, which is transferable to many fields beyond programming itself. These skills are highly valuable in domains such as data analysis, scientific research, finance, and even everyday decision-making.

Additionally, programming fosters creativity. It allows you to explore innovative ideas and experiment with different approaches. You have the freedom to invent and design solutions that others may not have thought of. This creative aspect of programming promotes innovation and can lead to groundbreaking advancements in technology.

The demand for programmers is continuously growing across industries. Companies of all sizes and sectors rely on software applications to streamline processes, reach customers, and gain a competitive edge. By learning programming, you equip yourself with a skill set that is in high demand, opening up a wide range of job opportunities and increasing your employability.

Furthermore, programming encourages collaboration and teamwork. Many projects require programmers to work together, combining their skills and expertise to achieve a common goal. Collaborative coding fosters communication, problem-solving, and a deeper understanding of different perspectives. It allows you to engage in the vibrant programming community, share ideas, and learn from others.

Learning programming is also a gateway to understanding and interacting with technology on a deeper level. It helps demystify the digital world and empowers you to be an informed user. You gain insights into how software applications work, which enhances your ability to troubleshoot issues, adapt to new technologies, and make informed decisions about the digital tools you use.

Lastly, programming provides lifelong learning opportunities. The field is constantly evolving, with new languages, frameworks, and technologies emerging regularly. Learning programming cultivates a growth mindset and a passion for continuous learning. It encourages you to stay curious, explore new concepts, and adapt to changing technological landscapes.

In conclusion, learning programming offers a multitude of benefits. It enables you to create, problem-solve, think critically, and collaborate effectively. It opens up career opportunities, nurtures creativity, deepens your understanding of technology, and encourages lifelong learning. Whether you aspire to be a professional programmer or simply want to gain a valuable skill, programming is a pathway to personal and professional growth in our increasingly digital world.

Common Programming Languages

There are numerous programming languages available, each with its own features, strengths, and areas of application. Here are some common programming languages you may come across:

Python: Python is a versatile and beginner-friendly language known for its readability and simplicity. It is widely used in web development, data analysis, artificial intelligence, scientific computing, and automation. Python's extensive libraries and frameworks make it a popular choice for various applications.

JavaScript: JavaScript is the language of the web. It is primarily used for front-end development, enabling interactive and dynamic web pages. JavaScript is also used in server-side development (Node.js), mobile app development, and game development.

Java: Java is a robust, object-oriented language that is widely used in enterprise-level applications, Android app development, and large-scale systems. It offers platform independence, strong community support, and extensive libraries and frameworks.

C++: C++ is a powerful and efficient language often used for system programming, game development, and high-performance applications. It provides low-level control, memory management, and is widely used in the field of computer graphics.

C#: C# (pronounced C sharp) is a language developed by Microsoft and is primarily used for developing Windows applications, game development using Unity, and building enterprise-level applications on the .NET framework.

Ruby: Ruby is a dynamic, object-oriented language known for its simplicity and readability. It is commonly used in web development frameworks such as Ruby on Rails and is favored for its productivity and elegant syntax.

PHP: PHP is a popular scripting language designed for web development. It is used for server-side scripting to build dynamic web pages and web applications. PHP is commonly integrated with HTML and works well with databases.

Swift: Swift is a modern programming language developed by Apple for iOS, macOS, watchOS, and tvOS app development. It is designed to be safe, fast, and expressive, providing a seamless development experience for Apple platforms.

TypeScript: TypeScript is a superset of JavaScript that adds static typing and additional features to JavaScript. It is widely adopted for large-scale JavaScript applications, providing enhanced type checking and tooling support.

Go: Go, also known as Golang, is a relatively new language developed by Google. It is designed for efficient concurrency, simplicity, and ease of use. Go is often used in backend development, cloud services, and system programming.

R: R is a language widely used for statistical computing and data analysis. It offers a vast array of specialized packages and tools for data manipulation, visualization, and statistical modeling. R is commonly used in fields such as data science, bioinformatics, and social sciences.

MATLAB: MATLAB is a high-level language and development environment commonly used in scientific and engineering disciplines. It is known for its extensive numerical computing capabilities, data visualization tools, and built-in libraries for various domains.

Rust: Rust is a systems programming language known for its emphasis on memory safety, performance, and concurrency. It provides strong memory management guarantees and is often used in areas where performance and reliability are critical, such as operating systems or embedded systems.

Kotlin: Kotlin is a modern, statically-typed language that runs on the Java Virtual Machine (JVM). It is officially supported for Android app development and offers concise syntax, null safety, and interoperability with Java. Kotlin has gained popularity due to its enhanced productivity and safety features.

Swift: Swift is a programming language developed by Apple for iOS, macOS, watchOS, and tvOS app development. It is designed to be easy to learn, safe, and efficient. Swift has become the preferred language for developing native applications on Apple platforms.

SQL: SQL (Structured Query Language) is a domain-specific language used for managing and manipulating relational databases. It allows for efficient retrieval, insertion, updating, and deletion of data. SQL is a fundamental skill for working with databases in various applications.

Perl: Perl is a versatile scripting language commonly used for text processing, system administration, and web development. It provides powerful regular expression capabilities and a rich set of built-in functions, making it suitable for various automation tasks.

Shell scripting: Shell scripting refers to writing scripts in scripting languages specific to command-line interfaces (e.g., Bash, PowerShell). Shell scripts are used for automating repetitive tasks, system administration, and executing command-line operations.

Scala: Scala is a modern, statically-typed language that runs on the Java Virtual Machine (JVM). It combines object-oriented and functional programming paradigms and is often used in big data processing frameworks like Apache Spark.

HTML/CSS: Although not considered traditional programming languages, HTML (Hypertext Markup Language) and CSS (Cascading Style Sheets) are fundamental for web development. HTML is used for structuring web pages, while CSS is used for styling and layout.

Remember, each programming language has its own strengths, features, and areas of application. The choice of language depends on the specific requirements of your project, the target platform, and the ecosystem surrounding the language.

It's important to note that this list represents only a fraction of the available programming languages. The choice of language depends on the specific project requirements, target platforms, personal preferences, and the ecosystem surrounding the language, including community support and available resources.

Setting Up Your Development Environment

Setting up your development environment is an important step before you start programming. It involves configuring the necessary tools and software to create, edit, compile, and run your code efficiently. Here's a general overview of setting up a development environment:

Choose an Operating System: Decide on the operating system you want to use for development, such as Windows, macOS, or Linux. Different programming languages and tools may have specific requirements or work best on certain operating systems, so consider the compatibility and support for your chosen language.

Install a Text Editor or Integrated Development Environment (IDE): A text editor or IDE is where you write and edit your code. Some popular choices include Visual Studio Code, Sublime Text, Atom, IntelliJ IDEA, and PyCharm. Install your preferred text editor/IDE, and customize it with themes and extensions as per your preference.

Install the Programming Language(s): Install the programming language(s) you plan to work with. Visit the official website of the programming language and follow the installation instructions. Many languages have pre-packaged distributions that include compilers, interpreters, and other necessary tools.

Set Up a Command-Line Interface (CLI): A CLI provides a text-based interface to interact with your development environment. This can be the native command prompt (e.g., Command Prompt on Windows, Terminal on macOS and Linux), or you can use specialized CLI tools such as PowerShell, Git Bash, or Oh My Zsh.

Install Version Control Software: Version control software, such as Git, helps track changes to your code, collaborate with others, and manage different versions of your project. Install Git by downloading it from the official website and follow the installation instructions.

Install Additional Tools and Libraries: Depending on your programming language and specific project requirements, you may need additional tools, libraries, or frameworks. These could include package managers (e.g., pip for Python, npm for

JavaScript), build systems (e.g., Maven, Gradle), and development libraries specific to your chosen language.

Configure your Environment: Once the necessary software is installed, you may need to configure your environment settings. This includes setting up environment variables, paths, and aliases to ensure that the command-line tools and compilers can be accessed easily.

Test Your Environment: After completing the setup, verify that your development environment is working correctly. Open your text editor or IDE, create a new file, write a basic "Hello, World!" program, and run it to ensure that the execution is successful.

Remember, the setup process may vary depending on your specific requirements and the programming language you are using. It is always a good idea to refer to the official documentation or online tutorials specific to your chosen language for detailed instructions on setting up the development environment.

Setting up a clean and efficient development environment can significantly enhance your productivity and ensure a smooth coding experience as you dive into programming.

Chapter 2: Fundamentals of Programming

Variables and Data Types

Variables and data types are fundamental concepts in programming that allow you to store and manipulate data within a program. Here's an explanation of variables and data types:

Variables:

In programming, a variable is a named container that holds a value or data. It acts as a placeholder for storing and accessing data during the execution of a program. Variables can be assigned a value, which can be changed and manipulated as the program runs.

To use a variable, you need to declare it, specifying its name and optionally its data type. For example, in Python, you can declare a variable like this:

```
my_variable = 10
```

In the above example, my_variable is the name of the variable, and 10 is the value assigned to it. You can later refer to my_variable to access or modify its value.

Data Types:

Data types define the nature of the data that can be stored in a variable. Different programming languages provide various data types, each with its characteristics and range of values. Common data types include:

Numeric Types:

Integer: Represents whole numbers (e.g., 10, -5, 0).

Floating-Point: Represents decimal numbers with fractional parts (e.g., 3.14, -0.5).

String: Represents a sequence of characters (e.g., "Hello, World!").

Boolean: Represents a logical value, either True or False, used for logical comparisons and branching.

Array/List: Represents an ordered collection of elements of the same type.

Dictionary/Map: Represents a collection of key-value pairs, where each key is associated with a value.

Tuple: Represents an immutable ordered collection of elements of different types.

Custom/User-Defined Types: Some programming languages allow you to define your own data types, such as classes and structures, which can have multiple properties and methods.

The choice of data type depends on the nature of the data you need to store and manipulate. It is important to select the appropriate data type to ensure efficient memory usage and accurate computations.

Programming languages often provide built-in functions or methods to convert data from one type to another, allowing you to perform operations and transformations on variables of different types.

Integer: An integer data type represents whole numbers without any fractional or decimal part. Depending on the programming language, integer data types may have different ranges, such as int (32-bit signed integer), long (64-bit signed integer), or short (16-bit signed integer). Examples of integer values include 5, -10, and 0.

Floating-Point: A floating-point data type represents numbers with a fractional or decimal part. It is used to store real numbers. Commonly used floating-point types are float (single-precision floating-point) and double (double-precision floating-point). Floating-point numbers are written with a decimal point, such as 3.14 or -0.5.

String: A string data type represents a sequence of characters. It is used to store textual data, such as names, sentences, or any other collection of characters. Strings are typically enclosed in quotation marks, such as "Hello, World!". In some languages, strings are immutable, meaning they cannot be changed after creation.

Boolean: A boolean data type represents a logical value that can be either True or False. It is used for logical comparisons, conditionals, and control flow in a program. Boolean values are useful for decision-making and branching based on specific conditions.

Array/List: An array or list data type is used to store a collection of elements. Arrays have a fixed size, while lists can dynamically grow or shrink. Elements within an array or list can be of the same or different data types. Arrays/lists are useful when working with a collection of related data, such as a list of numbers or names.

Dictionary/Map: A dictionary or map data type is used to store key-value pairs, where each key is associated with a value. Dictionaries/maps allow efficient lookup and retrieval of values based on their keys. They are useful for representing relationships or mappings between different entities.

Tuple: A tuple data type represents an ordered collection of elements of different types. Unlike arrays or lists, tuples are usually immutable, meaning their elements cannot be modified after creation. Tuples are useful for grouping related data together and passing multiple values as a single unit.

It's important to note that different programming languages may have additional data types or variations of the mentioned types. It's recommended to refer to the documentation or language-specific resources to understand the specific data types available in the language you are using.

Understanding variables and data types is crucial as they form the building blocks for writing programs that can handle and process data effectively. By declaring variables and utilizing appropriate data types, you can store, manipulate, and represent various kinds of information within your programs.

Operators and Expressions

Operators and expressions are fundamental elements of programming that allow you to perform operations and computations on data. They enable you to manipulate values, make comparisons, and perform various calculations. Let's explore operators and expressions in more detail:

Operators:

In programming, operators are symbols or keywords that perform specific operations on one or more operands (values or variables). Here are some common types of operators:

Arithmetic Operators:

Addition (+): Performs addition of two values.

Subtraction (-): Performs subtraction of one value from another.

Multiplication (*): Performs multiplication of two values.

Division (/): Performs division of one value by another.

Modulus (%): Computes the remainder after division.

Exponentiation (**): Raises a value to the power of another.

Assignment Operators:

Assignment (=): Assigns a value to a variable.

*Compound assignment operators (e.g., +=, -=, *=):* Combine an arithmetic operation with assignment.

Comparison Operators:

Equal to (==): Checks if two values are equal.

Not equal to (!=): Checks if two values are not equal.

Greater than (>), Less than (<): Checks the relative magnitude of values.

Greater than or equal to (>=), Less than or equal to (<=): Checks the relative magnitude or equality of values.

Logical Operators:

Logical AND (&&): Performs a logical AND operation on two conditions.

Logical OR (||): Performs a logical OR operation on two conditions.

Logical NOT (!): Negates a logical value.

Bitwise Operators:

Bitwise AND (&): Performs bitwise AND operation on two values.

Bitwise OR (|): Performs bitwise OR operation on two values.

Bitwise XOR (^): Performs bitwise exclusive OR operation on two values.

Bitwise NOT (~): Flips the bits of a value.

Expressions:

Expressions are combinations of values, variables, operators, and function calls that evaluate to a single value. Expressions can be as simple as a single value or as complex as a mathematical equation involving multiple operators and operands.

For example, consider the following expression:

```python
result = (2 + 3) * (7 - 4)
```

In this expression, the addition and subtraction operators are used to perform calculations, and the result is assigned to the variable result. The expression evaluates to the value 15.

Expressions can also include function calls and other more complex constructs. For instance:

```python
average = (sum(numbers)) / len(numbers)
```

In this expression, the sum() function is called to calculate the sum of a list of numbers. The sum is then divided by the length of the list to compute the average.

By combining operators and operands in expressions, you can perform a wide range of calculations, comparisons, and logical operations within your programs. Understanding and utilizing operators and expressions effectively allows you to manipulate and analyze data to achieve desired outcomes.

String Concatenation:

In many programming languages, the + operator is also used for string concatenation. It combines two or more strings together. For example:

```python
greeting = "Hello, " + "World!"
```

In this case, the + operator concatenates the two strings to produce the result "Hello, World!".

Increment and Decrement Operators:

Some programming languages provide increment (++) and decrement (--) operators, which increase or decrease the value of a variable by 1, respectively. For example:

```javascript
let count = 5;
count++;   // Increment by 1
console.log(count);   // Output: 6
```

Compound Assignment Operators:

Compound assignment operators combine an arithmetic operation with assignment. They are a shorthand way of performing an operation and updating the value of a variable simultaneously. Examples include += (addition and assignment), -= (subtraction and assignment), *= (multiplication and assignment), /= (division and assignment), and so on. For example:

```python
x = 5
x += 3  # Equivalent to: x = x + 3
```

Operator Precedence and Associativity:

Operators have different levels of precedence, which determines the order in which operations are performed in an expression. For example, in the expression 2 + 3 * 4, the multiplication is performed first due to its higher precedence, resulting in the value 14. Parentheses can be used to override the default precedence. Associativity determines the order of evaluation for operators with the same precedence. For example, the addition operator (+) is left associative, so 2 + 3 + 4 is evaluated as (2 + 3) + 4.

Ternary Operator:

The ternary operator is a shorthand way of writing an if-else statement in a single expression. It has the form: condition ? expression1 : expression2. If the condition is true, expression1 is evaluated; otherwise, expression2 is evaluated. For example:

```java
int age = 20;
String message = (age >= 18) ? "Adult" : "Minor";
```

Operator Overloading:

Some programming languages support operator overloading, which allows operators to behave differently depending on the types of the operands. For example, in Python, the + operator can be overloaded to concatenate strings or perform arithmetic addition, depending on the operand types.

Understanding the different types of operators, their behaviors, and operator precedence helps you construct meaningful expressions and perform calculations accurately in your programs. Proper use of operators and expressions is essential for manipulating data, making decisions, and controlling the flow of your code.

Control Flow: Conditionals and Loops

Control flow refers to the order in which statements are executed in a program. Conditionals and loops are essential control flow constructs that allow you to make decisions and repeat blocks of code based on certain conditions. Let's explore conditionals and loops in more detail:

Conditionals:

Conditionals enable you to make decisions in your code based on the evaluation of a condition. They allow you to execute different blocks of code depending on whether a condition is true or false. The most common conditional statements are:

If Statement:

The if statement allows you to execute a block of code only if a specified condition is true. If the condition is false, the block is skipped.

```python
if condition:
    # Code to be executed if condition is true
```

If-Else Statement:

The if-else statement provides an alternative block of code to execute when the condition is false.

```python
if condition:
    # Code to be executed if condition is true
else:
    # Code to be executed if condition is false
```

If-Elif-Else Statement:

The if-elif-else statement allows you to check multiple conditions sequentially and execute the corresponding block of code that corresponds to the first true condition.

```python
if condition1:
    # Code to be executed if condition1 is true
elif condition2:
    # Code to be executed if condition2 is true
else:
    # Code to be executed if all conditions are false
```

Loops:

Loops enable you to repeat a block of code multiple times until a certain condition is met. They provide a way to automate repetitive tasks and iterate over collections or ranges of values. The most common types of loops are:

While Loop:

The while loop repeatedly executes a block of code as long as a specified condition is true.

```python
while condition:
    # Code to be executed while condition is true
```

For Loop:

The for loop iterates over a sequence (e.g., a list, string, or range) and executes a block of code for each item in the sequence.

```python
for item in sequence:
    # Code to be executed for each item in the sequence
```

Nested Loops:

Loops can be nested within each other to perform more complex iterations. This is useful when you need to iterate over multiple dimensions or perform repetitive operations within a loop.

```python
for i in range(3):
    for j in range(3):
        # Code to be executed for each combination of i and j
```

Loop Control Statements:

Loop control statements allow you to modify the behavior of loops. Common control statements include break, which terminates the loop prematurely, and continue, which skips the rest of the current iteration and moves to the next iteration.

By using conditionals and loops, you can control the execution flow of your program and make it more dynamic and adaptable. Conditionals allow you to make decisions based on specific conditions, while loops enable you to repeat code until a condition is met. These control flow constructs provide flexibility and allow you to automate repetitive tasks and handle different scenarios in your code effectively.

Functions and Modularization

Functions and modularization are crucial concepts in programming that promote code organization, reusability, and maintainability. They allow you to break down your code into smaller, manageable parts and encapsulate logic into reusable units. Let's explore functions and modularization in more detail:

Functions:

Functions are self-contained blocks of code that perform a specific task or calculation. They take inputs (arguments) and can optionally return a result. Functions allow you to modularize your code by separating distinct tasks into reusable units. Here are key aspects of functions:

Function Declaration:

Functions are declared with a name, a set of parentheses that may contain input parameters, and a block of code that defines the function's behavior. For example:

```python
def greet(name):
    print("Hello, " + name)
```

To execute a function, you call it by its name and provide the required arguments. For example:

```python
greet("John")
```

Return Statement:

Functions can optionally return a value using the return statement. The returned value can be assigned to a variable or used in other parts of your code. For example:

```python
def add(a, b):
    return a + b

result = add(3, 5)  # result is assigned the value 8
```

Parameters and Arguments:

Functions can have parameters (also known as formal parameters) defined in their declaration, which act as placeholders for values passed into the function. Arguments are the actual values passed into the function when it is called. For example:

```python
def multiply(a, b):
    return a * b

product = multiply(4, 6)  # a is assigned 4, b is assigned 6
```

Modularization:

Modularization involves dividing a program into separate modules or units, allowing for better code organization, reuse, and maintainability. Functions play a crucial role in achieving modularization. Here are some benefits of modularization:

Reusability:

By encapsulating code within functions, you can reuse the same logic multiple times in different parts of your program. This saves time and effort, reduces code duplication, and promotes a more efficient development process.

Code Organization and Readability:

Functions help organize code by breaking it down into smaller, focused units. This makes code more readable, easier to understand, and allows for easier debugging and maintenance.

Abstraction and Encapsulation:

Functions enable you to abstract complex operations behind simple interfaces. By providing input parameters and returning results, functions hide the implementation details, allowing you to focus on the high-level behavior of the function.

Collaboration and Collaboration:

Modularization facilitates collaboration among team members. Different programmers can work on separate functions independently and integrate them into the larger program seamlessly. It also allows for code reuse across different projects.

Testing and Debugging:

Functions make it easier to test and debug code. Since functions encapsulate specific functionality, you can write focused tests for individual functions and isolate issues when debugging.

By utilizing functions and modularization, you can create more organized, reusable, and maintainable code. Functions allow you to break down complex tasks into manageable units, improve code readability, and promote collaboration and code reuse. Modularization enhances code organization and scalability, making it easier to maintain and expand your programs.

Chapter 3: Getting Started with a Language (e.g., Python)

Installing Python

To get started with Python programming, you'll need to install Python on your computer. The installation process is straightforward and involves a few simple steps.

First, visit the official Python website at python.org. On the website, you'll find different versions of Python available. It's generally recommended to choose the latest stable version, which is Python 3.x (e.g., Python 3.9).

Next, select the appropriate installer for your operating system. Python provides installers for Windows, macOS, and Linux. Choose the installer that matches your operating system, and click on the download link to begin the download.

Once the installer is downloaded, locate the file and run it. The installer will guide you through the installation process. It's usually best to accept the default settings unless you have specific preferences.

During the installation, you may have the option to customize certain settings. One important option is to add Python to the system's PATH. Enabling this option allows you to run Python commands from the command prompt or terminal easily.

After configuring the installation options, proceed with the installation. Follow the prompts and wait for the installation to complete. The installer will take care of copying the necessary files and setting up Python on your system.

Once the installation is finished, it's a good idea to verify that Python is installed correctly. Open a command prompt (Windows) or terminal (macOS/Linux) and type python --version. This command will display the installed Python version, confirming that the installation was successful. You can also run the python command to open the Python interactive shell, where you can directly type and execute Python commands.

Congratulations! With Python installed on your computer, you're now ready to start writing and running Python programs. You can use any text editor or integrated development environment (IDE) to write your Python code. Simply save your code with a .py extension and run it by executing the python command followed by the name of your Python file.

Installing Python is an essential first step towards learning and exploring the world of Python programming. It provides you with the necessary tools to write and execute Python code on your computer. Enjoy your Python programming journey!

Running Your First Program

Once you have Python installed on your computer, you're ready to write and run your first Python program. Follow these simple steps to get started:

Open a text editor: First, open a text editor or an integrated development environment (IDE) of your choice. Notepad (Windows), TextEdit (macOS), Visual Studio Code, or PyCharm are popular options.

Write your Python code: In the text editor, start by writing your Python code. For your first program, let's keep it simple. Type the following line:

```python
print("Hello, World!")
```

This code instructs Python to display the text "Hello, World!" on the screen.

Save your program: Save your program with a .py extension, such as "hello.py". The .py extension indicates that it's a Python file.

Open a command prompt or terminal: Open a command prompt (Windows) or terminal (macOS/Linux). This is where you'll run your Python program.

Navigate to the program's directory: Use the cd command (change directory) in the command prompt or terminal to navigate to the directory where you saved your Python program. For example, if your program is saved on the desktop, you would run:

```bash
cd Desktop
```

Run your Python program: Once you're in the correct directory, type the following command and press Enter:

```bash
python hello.py
```

This command tells Python to execute the code in the "hello.py" file.

Observe the output: After running the command, you should see the output of your program, which will be "Hello, World!" displayed on the screen.

Congratulations! You have successfully run your first Python program. This simple program demonstrates the basic structure of a Python program and the print() function, which is used to output information.

As you progress in your Python journey, you'll learn more about variables, control flow, and other features that will allow you to write more complex and interactive programs.

Remember to save your program after making any changes, and each time you want to run it again, navigate to the program's directory in the command prompt or terminal and execute the python command followed by the name of your Python file.

Enjoy exploring the world of Python programming and have fun experimenting with your own programs!

Input and Output

Input and output (I/O) are fundamental concepts in programming that involve receiving data from the user (input) and displaying information to the user (output). Input allows programs to interact with users, while output provides feedback and results. Here's an explanation of input and output in programming:

Input:

Input refers to receiving data or information from the user or an external source. It allows programs to accept user input and make decisions or perform operations based on that input. Here are common methods for accepting input:

Reading from the Keyboard:

Most programming languages provide functions or methods to read input from the keyboard. For example, in Python, the input() function is used to prompt the user for input and store the entered value in a variable. Here's an example:

```python
name = input("Enter your name: ")
```

Command-Line Arguments:

Programs can also accept input through command-line arguments. Command-line arguments are values passed to a program when it is run from the command line. The program can access these values and use them as input parameters.

File Input:

Programs can read input from external files. This is useful when you need to process large amounts of data or when the input is not directly entered by the user. The program reads the contents of the file and processes it accordingly.

Output:

Output involves displaying information or results to the user or writing it to an external file or device. Output provides feedback, results, or any necessary information generated by the program. Here are common methods for producing output:

Printing to the Console:

The print() function is commonly used to display output on the console or terminal. It accepts one or more arguments and prints them to the screen. For example, in Python:

```python
print("Hello, World!")
```

Writing to Files:

Programs can write output to external files. This is useful for storing results or generating reports. The program opens a file, writes the desired content, and then closes the file.

Displaying Graphics or User Interfaces:

In some cases, programs need to display graphical output or interact with users through a graphical user interface (GUI). Specific libraries or frameworks are used to handle such graphical output.

Input and output are crucial for creating interactive programs and allowing users to interact with software. By accepting user input, programs can tailor their behavior based on specific needs.

Output enables programs to provide meaningful information, results, or visual feedback to users.

When designing programs, it's important to consider input validation to handle potential errors or unexpected input from users. Additionally, formatting output in a clear and readable manner enhances the user experience.

Understanding and effectively utilizing input and output mechanisms allows you to create dynamic and interactive programs that can process data and provide meaningful feedback to users.

Variables and Data Types in Python

In Python, variables and data types play a fundamental role in storing and manipulating data. Variables serve as containers for holding values, while data types define the nature of the data that can be stored in variables. Let's explore variables and data types in Python:

Variables:

In Python, variables are created by assigning a value to a name. Unlike some other programming languages, you don't need to explicitly declare the variable's type. Python infers the type based on the assigned value. Here's an example of variable assignment in Python:

```python
name = "John"   # A variable named 'name' is assigned the string value "John"
age = 25        # A variable named 'age' is assigned the integer value 25
```

Data Types:

Python has several built-in data types that define the nature of the data stored in variables. The common data types in Python include:

Numeric Types:

Integer (int): Represents whole numbers (e.g., 10, -5, 0).

Floating-Point (float): Represents decimal numbers with fractional parts (e.g., 3.14, -0.5).

String (str):

Represents a sequence of characters (e.g., "Hello, World!").

Boolean (bool):

Represents a logical value, either True or False, used for logical comparisons and conditions.

List (list):

Represents an ordered collection of elements, which can be of different types. Lists are mutable (changeable) and enclosed in square brackets ([]).

Tuple (tuple):

Similar to lists, tuples represent ordered collections of elements. However, tuples are immutable (unchangeable) and enclosed in parentheses (()).

Dictionary (dict):

Represents a collection of key-value pairs. Each value is associated with a unique key. Dictionaries are enclosed in curly braces ({}) and are useful for storing and retrieving data based on keys.

Set (set):

Represents an unordered collection of unique elements. Sets are enclosed in curly braces ({}) or can be created using the set() function.

These are the basic data types in Python, and they can be combined and used in more complex ways.

Type Conversion:

Python provides built-in functions for converting data between different types. For example, you can use the int(), float(), str(), or bool() functions to convert data to the desired type.

```python
age = "25"  # A variable named 'age' is assigned the string value "25"

age_int = int(age)  # Convert the string to an integer using the int() function
```

Understanding variables and data types is essential for effectively working with data in Python. By assigning values to variables and utilizing appropriate data types, you can manipulate and process data efficiently in your programs.

Expressions in Python

Expressions in Python are combinations of values, variables, and operators that evaluate to a single value. They allow you to perform calculations and produce results. Expressions can be as simple as a single value or as complex as a mathematical equation involving multiple operators and operands.

For example, consider the following expression:

```python
result = (2 + 3) * (7 - 4)
```

In this expression, the addition and subtraction operators are used to perform calculations, and the result is assigned to the variable result. The expression evaluates to the value 15.

Expressions can also include function calls, variable assignments, and other more complex constructs. For instance:

```python
average = sum(numbers) / len(numbers)
```

In this expression, the sum() function is called to calculate the sum of a list of numbers. The sum is then divided by the length of the list to compute the average.

Understanding operators and expressions in Python allows you to perform calculations, comparisons, and logical operations effectively. By combining operators and operands, you can create powerful expressions that manipulate and analyze data in your programs.

Control Flow in Python

Control flow in Python refers to the order in which statements are executed in a program. It allows you to control the flow of execution based on certain conditions or iterate over blocks of code. Python provides several control flow constructs to achieve this. Let's explore them:

Conditional Statements (if, elif, else):

Conditional statements allow you to execute different blocks of code based on specific conditions. The basic structure includes an if statement followed by optional elif (short for "else if") statements and an optional else statement. Here's an example:

```python
if condition1:
    # Code to be executed if condition1 is true
elif condition2:
    # Code to be executed if condition2 is true
else:
    # Code to be executed if all conditions are false
```

The elif and else clauses are optional, and you can have multiple elif clauses if needed. The statements are evaluated sequentially, and only the first true condition's block is executed.

Loops:

Loops allow you to repeat a block of code multiple times or iterate over a sequence of items. Python provides two main types of loops: while loop: The while loop repeatedly executes a block of code as long as a specified condition is true. The condition is checked before each iteration. Here's an example:

```python
while condition:
    # Code to be executed while condition is true
```

for loop: The for loop iterates over a sequence of items, such as a list or a string, and executes a block of code for each item in the sequence. Here's an example:

```python
for item in sequence:
    # Code to be executed for each item in the sequence
```

The item variable takes on the value of each item in the sequence one by one, and the loop body is executed for each iteration.

Loops can be controlled using statements like break, which terminates the loop prematurely, and continue, which skips the current iteration and moves to the next.

Exception Handling (try, except, finally):

Exception handling allows you to catch and handle runtime errors and exceptional situations in your code. The try block is used to enclose the code that may raise an exception. If an exception occurs, it is caught by the corresponding except block. You can also include an optional finally block that executes regardless of whether an exception was raised. Here's an example:

```python
try:
    # Code that may raise an exception
except ExceptionType:
    # Code to handle the exception
finally:
    # Code to be executed regardless of exceptions
```

Multiple except blocks can be used to handle different types of exceptions, allowing you to provide specific error handling for different scenarios.

Control flow constructs provide flexibility and allow you to control the execution path of your program. They enable you to make decisions based on conditions, repeat code as needed, and handle exceptional situations gracefully. By utilizing these constructs effectively, you can create more dynamic and interactive programs in Python.

Chapter 4: Working with Data Structures

Arrays and Lists

In Python, arrays and lists are used to store collections of elements. They allow you to group related data together and perform operations on the entire collection. While they serve similar purposes, there are some differences between arrays and lists in Python. Let's explore arrays and lists:

Lists:

A list in Python is an ordered collection of elements enclosed in square brackets ([]). Here are some key characteristics of lists:

Mutable: Lists are mutable, meaning you can modify their elements. You can add, remove, or modify elements after the list is created.

Heterogeneous Elements: Lists can store elements of different data types. For example, a list can contain integers, strings, and even other lists.

Dynamic Size: Lists can dynamically grow or shrink as elements are added or removed. There is no fixed size limit for lists.

Accessing Elements: Elements in a list can be accessed using indexing. Indexing starts from 0, so the first element is at index 0, the second element is at index 1, and so on.

Common List Operations: Lists support various operations, such as appending elements, removing elements, concatenating lists, slicing, and more.

Here's an example of a list in Python:

```python
fruits = ["apple", "banana", "orange"]
```

Arrays:

In Python, arrays are provided by the array module. Unlike lists, arrays are used to store elements of the same data type. Some key aspects of arrays are:

Homogeneous Elements: Arrays can store elements of a single data type, such as integers, floats, or characters. This makes them more memory-efficient than lists.

Fixed Size: Arrays have a fixed size, meaning you need to specify the size when creating an array. Once created, the size cannot be changed.

Efficient Element Access: Since arrays have a fixed size and elements are of the same type, accessing elements in an array is generally faster compared to accessing elements in a list.

To use arrays in Python, you need to import the array module. Here's an example:

```python
from array import array

numbers = array('i', [1, 2, 3, 4, 5])  # Creates an array of integers
```

Arrays are useful when you need to work with large amounts of homogeneous data and require efficient element access.

In Python, lists are more commonly used due to their flexibility and the availability of built-in operations and functionalities. However, if you have specific requirements for homogeneous data storage and need better performance, you can consider using arrays from the array module.

Strings

In Python, a string is a sequence of characters enclosed in either single quotes (") or double quotes (""). Strings are one of the most commonly used data types in programming, and they allow you to represent and manipulate textual data. Here are some important aspects of strings in Python:

Creating Strings:

You can create a string by enclosing characters within quotes. For example:

```python
message = "Hello, World!"
```

String Manipulation:

Python provides various built-in string manipulation methods and operations. You can concatenate strings using the + operator, access individual characters using indexing, and use functions like len() to get the length of a string.

String Indexing and Slicing:

Strings are indexed, and you can access individual characters using square brackets and the index position. Indexing starts from 0, so the first character is at index 0, the second at index 1, and so on. For example:

```python
message = "Hello"
print(message[0])  # Output: 'H'
```

Slicing allows you to extract a portion of a string. It is done by specifying the start and end positions, separated by a colon. The end position is exclusive, meaning the character at that position is not included. For example:

```python
message = "Hello, World!"
print(message[0:5])  # Output: 'Hello'
```

String Methods:

Python provides numerous built-in string methods to manipulate and transform strings. Some commonly used methods include lower(), upper(), split(), strip(), replace(), startswith(), endswith(), and more.

String Concatenation:

Strings can be concatenated using the + operator or by placing them next to each other. For example:

```python
first_name = "John"
last_name = "Doe"
full_name = first_name + " " + last_name
```

String Formatting:

Python provides different methods for formatting strings, such as using the % operator, the format() method, or f-strings (formatted string literals). These methods allow you to incorporate variables or values into a string in a specific format.

String Immutability:

Strings in Python are immutable, meaning you cannot change individual characters within a string. However, you can create new strings by manipulating existing ones.

Understanding strings and their manipulation methods is essential for working with textual data in Python. They are used extensively in tasks such as input/output, text processing, data cleaning, and more. By utilizing the various string operations and methods available, you can effectively manipulate and analyze text in your Python programs.

Dictionaries and Sets

In Python, dictionaries and sets are two built-in data structures that allow you to store collections of elements. They are useful for organizing and manipulating data in different ways. Let's explore dictionaries and sets:

Dictionaries:

Dictionaries, often referred to as "dicts," are unordered collections of key-value pairs enclosed in curly braces ({ }). Here are some key characteristics of dictionaries:

Key-Value Mapping: Each element in a dictionary consists of a key and its corresponding value. The key acts as a unique identifier for the associated value.

Mutable: Dictionaries are mutable, meaning you can add, modify, or remove key-value pairs after the dictionary is created.

Accessing Elements: Elements in a dictionary are accessed using their keys. You can retrieve the value of a specific key by specifying the key in square brackets ([]). If the key is not present, it raises a KeyError.

No Duplicate Keys: Dictionary keys must be unique. If you assign a value to an existing key, it will update the value associated with that key.

Here's an example of a dictionary in Python:

```python
student = {
    "name": "John",
    "age": 25,
    "grade": "A"
}
```

Sets:

Sets are unordered collections of unique elements enclosed in curly braces ({ }) or created using the set() function. Here are some key characteristics of sets:

Unique Elements: Sets contain only unique elements. Duplicate elements are automatically removed.

Mutable: Sets are mutable, allowing you to add or remove elements after the set is created.

Mathematical Set Operations: Sets support mathematical set operations like union, intersection, and difference, which can be useful for combining or comparing multiple sets.

No Indexing: Elements in a set are not indexed, meaning you cannot access elements using indexing or slicing.

Here's an example of a set in Python:

```python
fruits = {"apple", "banana", "orange"}
```

Dictionaries and sets are powerful data structures that offer different capabilities. Dictionaries are useful when you need to associate values with unique keys and retrieve them efficiently. Sets, on the other hand, are beneficial when you want to store unique elements and perform set operations.

Both dictionaries and sets are versatile and widely used in various programming scenarios. Understanding their properties and methods allows you to organize and manipulate data effectively in your Python programs.

Tuples

In Python, a tuple is an ordered collection of elements enclosed in parentheses ( ) or created without any enclosing symbols. Tuples are similar to lists, but with one significant difference: they are immutable, meaning their elements cannot be modified once the tuple is created. Here are some key characteristics of tuples:

Creating Tuples:

Tuples can be created by enclosing elements in parentheses. For example:

```python
my_tuple = (1, 2, 3)
```

Alternatively, you can create a tuple without parentheses by separating the elements with commas. For example:

```python
my_tuple = 1, 2, 3
```

Immutable:

Tuples are immutable, which means you cannot modify individual elements or add/remove elements after the tuple is created. However, you can create new tuples by concatenating existing tuples or by using tuple-specific methods.

Ordered and Indexing:

Tuples maintain the order of elements, similar to lists. You can access individual elements using indexing, starting from 0. For example:

```python
my_tuple = ("apple", "banana", "orange")
print(my_tuple[0])  # Output: "apple"
```

Heterogeneous Elements:

Tuples can contain elements of different data types. For example, a tuple can include integers, strings, floats, or even other tuples.

Multiple Assignment and Unpacking:

Tuples support multiple assignment, allowing you to assign multiple variables at once using a single tuple. For example:

```python
x, y, z = (1, 2, 3)
```

Tuples can also be unpacked, where the elements of a tuple are assigned to multiple variables. This is useful when returning multiple values from a function or when working with tuples containing different pieces of information.

Use Cases:

Tuples are often used when you want to represent a collection of related, immutable values, such as coordinates, database records, or dates.

Tuples provide a way to group related data together while ensuring that the data cannot be modified accidentally. Their immutability makes them suitable for situations where you want to store constant or unchanging data. However, if you need to modify or manipulate the elements, consider using lists instead.

By understanding tuples and their properties, you can effectively use them to represent and work with ordered, immutable collections of elements in your Python programs.

Working with Data Structures in Python

Working with data structures in Python allows you to organize, manipulate, and analyze data efficiently. Python provides several built-in data structures that serve different purposes. Let's explore some commonly used data structures and their functionalities:

Lists:

Lists are versatile data structures that allow you to store and manipulate collections of elements. They are ordered and mutable, meaning you can modify, add, or remove elements. Lists support indexing, slicing, and a variety of methods for adding, removing, or manipulating elements.

Tuples:

Tuples are similar to lists but are immutable, meaning their elements cannot be modified once created. Tuples are commonly used when you want to represent a collection of related, unchanging values. They are often used for tasks such as returning multiple values from a function or representing coordinates.

Dictionaries:

Dictionaries are key-value pairs that allow you to store and retrieve values based on unique keys. They are unordered and mutable. Dictionaries are useful for mapping and associating related data. They provide fast lookup and retrieval of values based on keys.

Sets:

Sets are unordered collections of unique elements. They are mutable and support mathematical set operations such as union, intersection, and difference. Sets are useful when you want to perform operations like removing duplicates or checking membership efficiently.

Arrays:

Arrays are provided by the array module in Python. They are similar to lists but are more efficient for storing homogeneous data, such as numeric values. Arrays require a fixed size and allow fast element access and manipulation.

Strings:

Strings are used to represent and manipulate text data. They are immutable sequences of characters. Strings have various methods for manipulation, searching, and formatting. They are often used for tasks like data cleaning, text processing, and output generation.

These built-in data structures provide a solid foundation for working with different types of data in Python. Depending on your specific needs, you can choose the appropriate data structure to organize and manipulate your data effectively.

In addition to the built-in data structures, Python also provides powerful libraries and modules for advanced data structures and data manipulation, such as NumPy (for numerical computing), pandas (for data analysis), and more. These libraries extend the capabilities of Python and enable efficient handling of large datasets, complex computations, and data manipulation tasks.

By understanding and utilizing these data structures, you can write efficient, organized, and scalable code to work with different types of data in Python.

Chapter 5: Object-Oriented Programming (OOP) Basics

Introduction to OOP

Object-Oriented Programming (OOP) is a programming paradigm that focuses on organizing code around objects that encapsulate data and behavior. It provides a way to structure and design software systems based on real-world entities and their interactions. OOP promotes modular, reusable, and maintainable code. Here's an introduction to the key concepts in OOP:

Objects:

Objects are instances of a class and represent real-world entities or concepts. They encapsulate data (attributes) and behavior (methods). For example, in a car simulation, a Car class can represent the blueprint, while each actual car on the road would be an object of that class.

Classes:

Classes are blueprints or templates for creating objects. They define the structure, attributes, and behavior that objects of that class possess. A class serves as a blueprint for creating multiple instances (objects) with similar characteristics.

Encapsulation:

Encapsulation is the process of bundling data and related behavior together within an object. It allows data to be accessed and modified only through designated methods, ensuring data integrity and security.

Inheritance:

Inheritance is a mechanism that allows a class to inherit properties and behavior from another class. The class that inherits is called a subclass or derived class, while the class being inherited from is called the superclass or base class. Inheritance promotes code reuse and supports hierarchical relationships between classes.

Polymorphism:

Polymorphism allows objects of different classes to be treated as instances of a common superclass. It enables methods with the same name to be called on different objects, and the behavior of the method is determined based on the actual object type. Polymorphism promotes flexibility and extensibility in code.

Abstraction:

Abstraction focuses on providing simplified, high-level representations of complex systems. It allows you to hide unnecessary details and expose only relevant information and functionalities. Abstraction helps in building modular and maintainable code.

Modularity:

Modularity is the principle of breaking down a system into smaller, self-contained modules or components. Each module focuses on a specific task or responsibility, making the overall system easier to understand, maintain, and update.

OOP enables developers to model complex systems more intuitively, manage code complexity, and build reusable components. By organizing code around objects and their interactions, OOP promotes code reusability, flexibility, and scalability. It is widely used in software development for its ability to create modular, maintainable, and extensible applications.

In Python, OOP is supported natively, allowing you to create classes, define objects, and utilize the concepts of encapsulation, inheritance, polymorphism, and abstraction in your code.

Classes and Objects

In object-oriented programming (OOP), classes and objects are key concepts that form the building blocks of the program structure. Here's an explanation of classes and objects:

Classes:

A class is a blueprint or template that defines the attributes (data) and behaviors (methods) that objects of that class will possess. It provides a way to encapsulate related data and functionality into a single entity. Think of a class as a blueprint for creating objects with similar characteristics.

Class definitions in Python typically include member variables (attributes) and member functions (methods) that define the behavior of objects created from the class.

Here's an example of a simple class in Python:

```python
class Car:
    def __init__(self, make, model):
        self.make = make
        self.model = model


    def drive(self):
        print("The car is driving.")
```

In this example, the Car class has attributes make and model, and a method drive().

Objects:

An object is an instance of a class. It represents a specific entity or instance that has its own unique data and can perform actions defined by the class. Objects are created using the class as a blueprint.

When you create an object, it has access to the attributes and methods defined in its class. Each object can have different values for its attributes, while the methods are shared among all objects of the same class.

To create an object from a class, you use the class name followed
by parentheses:

```python
my_car = Car("Toyota", "Camry")
```

In this example, my_car is an object of the Car class. It has its
own make and model attributes, and it can perform the drive()
method.

You can access attributes and methods of an object using dot
notation:

```python
print(my_car.make)   # Output: "Toyota"
my_car.drive()   # Output: "The car is driving."
```

In OOP, classes provide a way to structure code by grouping
related data and behavior together. Objects created from those
classes allow you to work with specific instances and manipulate

their data and behavior as needed. This modular approach
promotes code reuse, flexibility, and maintainability.

Inheritance and Polymorphism

Inheritance and polymorphism are two key concepts in object-oriented programming (OOP) that promote code reuse, extensibility, and flexibility. Let's explore inheritance and polymorphism:

Inheritance:

Inheritance is a mechanism in OOP that allows a class to inherit properties and behaviors from another class. The class that inherits is called the subclass or derived class, and the class being inherited from is called the superclass or base class.

The subclass inherits all the attributes and methods of the superclass, allowing it to reuse and extend the functionality defined in the superclass.

Inheritance promotes code reuse, reduces redundancy, and supports hierarchical relationships between classes.

Here's an example of inheritance in Python:

```python
class Animal:
    def __init__(self, name):
        self.name = name

    def speak(self):
        print("The animal speaks.")


class Dog(Animal):
    def wag_tail(self):
        print("The dog wags its tail.")


my_dog = Dog("Buddy")
print(my_dog.name)  # Output: "Buddy"
my_dog.speak()  # Output: "The animal speaks."
my_dog.wag_tail()  # Output: "The dog wags its tail."
```

In this example, the Animal class is the superclass, and the Dog class is the subclass. The Dog class inherits the name attribute and speak() method from the Animal class. Additionally, it defines its own method wag_tail(). The object my_dog is an instance of the Dog class, which can access both the inherited and its own methods.

Polymorphism:

Polymorphism means "many forms" and refers to the ability of objects to take on different forms or behaviors based on their context or the way they are used.

In OOP, polymorphism allows objects of different classes to be treated as instances of a common superclass. This means that objects can be used interchangeably, and the appropriate method is called based on the actual object type at runtime.

Polymorphism enables code flexibility, extensibility, and modularity.

Here's an example of polymorphism in Python:

```python
class Animal:
    def __init__(self, name):
        self.name = name

    def speak(self):
        print("The animal speaks.")


class Dog(Animal):
    def speak(self):
        print("The dog barks.")


class Cat(Animal):
    def speak(self):
        print("The cat meows.")


def make_animal_speak(animal):
    animal.speak()
```

```python
dog = Dog("Buddy")
cat = Cat("Whiskers")

make_animal_speak(dog)  # Output: "The dog barks."
make_animal_speak(cat)  # Output: "The cat meows."
```

In this example, the Animal class has a speak() method. Both the Dog and Cat classes inherit from the Animal class and override the speak() method with their own implementation. The make_animal_speak() function takes an Animal object as a parameter and calls its speak() method. By passing different objects (a dog and a cat), the appropriate speak() method is called based on the actual object type, demonstrating polymorphism.

Inheritance and polymorphism are powerful concepts in OOP that allow for code reuse, flexibility, and the ability to work with objects interchangeably. They contribute to building modular and extensible systems in which objects can exhibit different behaviors based on their types and relationships.

Encapsulation and Abstraction

Encapsulation and abstraction are two important concepts in object-oriented programming (OOP) that help in designing modular and maintainable code. Let's explore encapsulation and abstraction:

Encapsulation:

Encapsulation is the bundling of related data (attributes) and behavior (methods) into a single unit called an object. It allows data to be accessed and modified only through well-defined methods or functions, known as getters and setters or accessors and mutators.

Encapsulation provides data hiding, which means that the internal implementation details of an object are hidden from the external world. This protects the integrity of the data and ensures that it is accessed and modified only in controlled ways.

Encapsulation promotes code maintainability, as changes to the internal implementation of an object do not affect other parts of the code that use the object's public interface.

Here's an example of encapsulation in Python:

```python
class BankAccount:
    def __init__(self, account_number, balance):
        self.account_number = account_number
        self.balance = balance

    def get_balance(self):
        return self.balance

    def deposit(self, amount):
        self.balance += amount

    def withdraw(self, amount):
        if amount <= self.balance:
            self.balance -= amount
        else:
            print("Insufficient funds.")


account = BankAccount("123456789", 1000)
print(account.get_balance())  # Output: 1000
account.deposit(500)
print(account.get_balance())  # Output: 1500
account.withdraw(2000)  # Output: "Insufficient funds."
```

In this example, the BankAccount class encapsulates the account
number and balance attributes. The get_balance() method allows
controlled access to the balance attribute, while the deposit() and

withdraw() methods provide controlled ways to modify the balance.

Abstraction:

Abstraction focuses on providing a simplified and high-level representation of complex systems. It involves hiding unnecessary implementation details and exposing only the essential features or functionalities of an object or system.

Abstraction allows you to create abstract classes or interfaces that define the common behavior or contract for a group of related objects. The concrete subclasses then provide the specific implementation details.

Abstraction helps in managing complexity, enhances code modularity, and allows you to work at a higher level of understanding without worrying about the low-level implementation details.

Here's an example of abstraction in Python:

```python
from abc import ABC, abstractmethod

class Shape(ABC):
    @abstractmethod
    def area(self):
        pass

class Rectangle(Shape):
    def __init__(self, length, width):
        self.length = length
        self.width = width

    def area(self):
        return self.length * self.width

class Circle(Shape):
    def __init__(self, radius):
        self.radius = radius

    def area(self):
        return 3.14 * self.radius**2
```

```python
rect = Rectangle(4, 5)
print(rect.area())  # Output: 20

circle = Circle(3)
print(circle.area())  # Output: 28.26
```

In this example, the Shape class is an abstract class that defines the common behavior for different shapes. The area() method is abstract, meaning it is defined but not implemented in the abstract class. The Rectangle and Circle classes are concrete implementations of the Shape class and provide the specific implementation for the area() method.

Abstraction allows you to work with objects at a higher level of abstraction, focusing on their essential features and behaviors, without worrying about the underlying implementation details.

Encapsulation and abstraction are fundamental principles in OOP that promote code organization, maintainability, and modularity.

By encapsulating related data and behavior into objects and providing abstract interfaces, you can create robust and scalable software systems.

OOP in Python

Object-Oriented Programming (OOP) is fully supported in Python and is widely used for developing complex and modular applications. Python provides the necessary features to create classes, define objects, and implement the key principles of OOP. Here's an overview of how OOP is implemented in Python:

Defining Classes:

Classes in Python are defined using the class keyword, followed by the class name, and a colon. The class definition can include attributes (data) and methods (functions).

Here's an example of a simple class definition in Python:

python

Copy code

```python
class Person:
    def __init__(self, name, age):
        self.name = name
        self.age = age
```

    def greet(self):

        print(f"Hello, my name is {self.name} and I'm {self.age} years old.")

Creating Objects:

Objects are instances of a class. They are created by calling the class as if it were a function, with optional arguments to initialize the object's attributes.

Here's an example of creating objects from the Person class:

python

Copy code

```python
person1 = Person("Alice", 30)

person2 = Person("Bob", 25)
```

Accessing Attributes and Calling Methods:

Once objects are created, you can access their attributes using dot notation (object.attribute) and call their methods using parentheses (object.method()).

Here's an example of accessing attributes and calling a method:

python

Copy code

```
print(person1.name)  # Output: "Alice"

person2.greet()  # Output: "Hello, my name is Bob and I'm 25 years old."
```

Inheritance:

Inheritance allows classes to inherit attributes and methods from a superclass (base class) to a subclass (derived class).

To create a subclass, you define it using the class keyword, followed by the subclass name and the superclass name in parentheses.

Here's an example of inheritance in Python:

python
Copy code

```python
class Student(Person):
    def __init__(self, name, age, student_id):
        super().__init__(name, age)
        self.student_id = student_id


    def study(self):
        print(f"{self.name} is studying.")


student = Student("Charlie", 20, "12345")
student.greet()  # Output: "Hello, my name is Charlie and I'm 20 years old."
student.study()  # Output: "Charlie is studying."
```

Polymorphism:

Polymorphism allows objects of different classes to be treated as instances of a common superclass. This allows you to write code that can work with objects interchangeably based on their common interface.

Polymorphism in Python is achieved by defining methods with the same name in different classes and calling them on objects of those classes.

Here's an example of polymorphism in Python:

python

Copy code

```python
def describe(person):
    person.greet()


describe(person1)  # Output: "Hello, my name is Alice and I'm 30 years old."
describe(student)  # Output: "Hello, my name is Charlie and I'm 20 years old."
```

Python's support for OOP allows you to create modular and reusable code by encapsulating data and behavior into classes and objects. With inheritance and polymorphism, you can establish relationships between classes and create flexible and extensible systems. OOP in Python promotes code organization,

maintainability, and code reuse, making it a powerful paradigm
for software development.

Chapter 6: Error Handling and Debugging

Common Types of Errors

In programming, errors can occur during code execution, and they are crucial for identifying and fixing issues in your programs. Here are some common types of errors that you may encounter:

Syntax Errors:

Syntax errors occur when the code violates the rules of the programming language syntax. It could be a missing parenthesis, a misplaced operator, or a misspelled keyword. These errors are detected by the compiler or interpreter during the parsing phase and prevent the code from running.

Runtime Errors (Exceptions):

Runtime errors, also known as exceptions, occur during the execution of a program. They indicate exceptional conditions that cannot be handled by the normal flow of the program. Common examples include division by zero, accessing an out-of-bounds array index, or calling a method on an object that doesn't exist.

Runtime errors can cause the program to terminate abruptly unless they are handled through exception handling mechanisms.

Logical Errors:

Logical errors, also called semantic errors, occur when the code does not produce the expected output or behavior due to flaws in the program's logic. These errors may not be detected by the compiler or interpreter since the syntax is correct, but they can lead to incorrect results or unintended behavior. Debugging techniques such as code inspection, test cases, and logical reasoning are usually employed to identify and fix logical errors.

Name Errors:

Name errors occur when a name or variable is used before it is defined or outside its scope. This can happen if a variable is misspelled, not declared, or out of scope. It is important to ensure that all names and variables are properly declared and within the appropriate scope.

Type Errors:

Type errors occur when an operation is performed on an object of an incompatible type. For example, trying to concatenate a string with an integer or calling a method that expects a certain type of argument but receiving a different type. Type errors can often be resolved by ensuring that the operands or arguments are of the correct type.

Attribute Errors:

Attribute errors occur when an attribute or method is accessed on an object that does not have that attribute or method. It can happen when attempting to access an undefined attribute or calling a method that is not available for a particular object. It is important to ensure that the object being accessed has the desired attribute or method.

To handle and resolve these errors, techniques such as debugging, logging, and error handling mechanisms like try-except blocks can be employed. By identifying and addressing these errors, you can improve the functionality, reliability, and robustness of your programs.

Debugging Techniques and Tools

Debugging is the process of identifying and resolving errors, bugs, and unexpected behaviors in your code. It involves investigating the root cause of the problem and making corrections to ensure that the code functions as intended. Here are some common debugging techniques and tools that can help in the debugging process:

Print Statements:

Inserting print statements in your code to display the values of variables, the flow of execution, and important checkpoints can help you understand the behavior of your code and identify issues. Print statements can be used to track the values of variables at different points in the program.

Debugging Statements:

Most programming languages provide debugging statements or functions that allow you to pause the execution of the code and inspect the program's state. For example, Python's pdb module provides a built-in debugger that allows you to step through the code line by line, set breakpoints, and examine variables.

Logging:

Logging is a technique where you write messages to a log file or console to track the flow of execution and important information during runtime. It allows you to record specific events, errors, or values, which can help in understanding the behavior of your code and identifying issues.

IDE Debugging Tools:

Integrated Development Environments (IDEs) often provide advanced debugging tools that can assist in identifying and resolving issues. These tools include features like breakpoints, stepping through code, inspecting variables, and analyzing call stacks. Popular IDEs like PyCharm, Visual Studio Code, and Eclipse have robust debugging capabilities.

Error Messages and Stack Traces:

When an error occurs during program execution, error messages and stack traces are generated, providing information about the error and the sequence of function calls that led to the error. Analyzing error messages and stack traces can help pinpoint the source of the error and guide you in fixing it.

Unit Testing:

Writing unit tests can help identify and isolate specific issues in your code. By creating tests that cover different scenarios and expected behaviors, you can verify the correctness of your code and detect regressions when changes are made.

Code Inspection and Review:

Taking a step back and carefully inspecting your code, reviewing the logic, and scrutinizing the algorithms can help identify logical errors or mistakes. Sometimes, a fresh perspective or the input of a colleague can uncover issues that were overlooked.

Debugging Tools and Libraries:

Depending on the programming language and platform, there are various debugging tools and libraries available that offer additional functionality for identifying and fixing bugs. These tools often provide features like code profiling, memory allocation tracking, and performance analysis.

Breakpoints:

Breakpoints allow you to pause the execution of your code at a specific line or condition. They enable you to examine the program's state, inspect variables, and step through the code line by line. IDEs and debuggers provide convenient ways to set breakpoints and navigate through the code during debugging.

Conditional Breakpoints:

Conditional breakpoints are breakpoints that are triggered only when a specific condition is met. This can be useful when you want to pause the execution at a certain point in the code based on a specific state or value.

Debugging Profilers:

Profilers help analyze the performance of your code by providing insights into its execution time, memory usage, and function call statistics. Profiling tools can help you identify bottlenecks and areas that need optimization.

Remote Debugging:

Remote debugging allows you to debug code running on a remote server or device. It enables you to connect to a remote environment and debug the code as if it were running locally. This is particularly useful for troubleshooting issues that occur in a different environment than your development machine.

Documentation and Online Resources:

Utilize documentation and online resources related to the programming language, frameworks, or libraries you are using. These resources often provide troubleshooting guides, FAQs, and community forums where you can find solutions to common issues or seek help from experienced developers.

Rubber Duck Debugging:

Rubber duck debugging is a technique where you explain your code and the problem you are facing to an inanimate object, such as a rubber duck. The process of explaining the code step by step can often help you identify the issue or uncover overlooked mistakes.

Collaborative Debugging:

Sometimes, a fresh set of eyes can be immensely helpful in debugging. Engage with your colleagues or join online communities to discuss the issue you are facing. Sharing code snippets, error messages, and observations can lead to valuable insights and potential solutions.

Remember that debugging is a skill that improves with practice and experience. By utilizing these techniques and tools, you can effectively identify and resolve issues in your code, leading to more reliable and efficient software development.

Exception Handling in Python

Exception handling in Python allows you to catch and handle errors or exceptional conditions that occur during the execution of your program. By handling exceptions, you can gracefully recover from errors, prevent program crashes, and provide informative error messages to users. Here's an overview of exception handling in Python:

try-except Block:

The try-except block is used to handle exceptions. It consists of a try block followed by one or more except blocks.

The code within the try block is executed, and if an exception occurs, it is caught by the corresponding except block that handles that particular type of exception.

Here's a simple example:

```python
try:
    # Code that may raise an exception
    result = 10 / 0  # Division by zero raises ZeroDivisionError
except ZeroDivisionError:
    # Exception handling code
    print("Error: Division by zero occurred.")
```

Multiple Except Blocks:

You can have multiple except blocks to handle different types of exceptions that may occur within the try block.

The except block with a matching exception type will be executed when that specific exception occurs.

Here's an example handling multiple exceptions:

```python
try:
    # Code that may raise an exception
    result = int("abc")  # Raises ValueError
except ZeroDivisionError:
    # Exception handling for ZeroDivisionError
    print("Error: Division by zero occurred.")
except ValueError:
    # Exception handling for ValueError
    print("Error: Invalid conversion to integer.")
```

Handling Multiple Exceptions in a Single Except Block:

You can handle multiple exceptions in a single except block by specifying the exception types within parentheses.

This approach is useful when you want to handle multiple exceptions in the same way.

Here's an example:

```python
try:
    # Code that may raise an exception
    result = int("abc")  # Raises ValueError
except (ZeroDivisionError, ValueError):
    # Exception handling for ZeroDivisionError and ValueError
    print("Error: An error occurred.")
```

Optional else Block:

The else block can be included after all the except blocks and is executed if no exceptions occur within the try block.

It is often used to specify code that should run when no exceptions are raised.

Here's an example:

```python
try:
    # Code that may raise an exception
    result = 10 / 2
except ZeroDivisionError:
    # Exception handling for ZeroDivisionError
    print("Error: Division by zero occurred.")
else:
    # Code to execute when no exceptions occur
    print("The result is:", result)
```

finally Block:

The finally block is an optional block that is executed regardless of whether an exception occurs or not.

It is typically used to specify cleanup code, such as closing files or releasing resources, that should always run.

Here's an example:

```python
try:
    # Code that may raise an exception
    result = open("myfile.txt", "r")
    # Perform some operations with the file
except FileNotFoundError:
    # Exception handling for FileNotFoundError
    print("Error: File not found.")
finally:
    # Cleanup code
    result.close()
```

Raising Exceptions:

You can raise exceptions explicitly using the raise statement. This allows you to create your own custom exceptions or raise built-in exceptions in specific scenarios.

Here's an example of raising a custom exception:

```python
try:
    # Code that may raise an exception
    age = int(input("Enter your age: "))
    if age < 0:
        raise ValueError("Age cannot be negative.")
except ValueError as e:
    # Exception handling for ValueError
    print("Error:", str(e))
```

By using try-except blocks, you can handle exceptions, prevent program crashes, and provide meaningful error messages to users. It allows you to gracefully handle exceptional situations and guide the program flow based on specific conditions.

Best Practices for Debugging

Debugging is an essential part of the software development process. It helps identify and resolve issues in your code, ensuring that it functions correctly. Here are some best practices for effective debugging:

Understand the Expected Behavior:

Before diving into debugging, make sure you have a clear understanding of the expected behavior of your code. Refer to the requirements, specifications, or documentation to ensure you have a solid understanding of what the code is supposed to do.

Reproduce the Issue:

Ensure that you can reproduce the issue consistently. Identify the specific steps or conditions that trigger the problem. Having a reliable reproduction case helps in isolating and resolving the bug effectively.

Use Version Control:

Utilize version control systems like Git to manage your codebase. By committing changes frequently, you can revert to a known working state if a bug is introduced. Version control also helps track code changes and collaborate with other developers.

Divide and Conquer:

Narrow down the problem area by using a systematic approach. Isolate the code section where the bug is occurring. Divide the code into smaller parts, test them individually, and gradually narrow down the problem area. This process helps identify the root cause more efficiently.

Analyze Error Messages and Logs:

Error messages and logs provide valuable information about the issue. Analyze them carefully to understand the nature of the problem, identify the location of the error, and gather relevant details such as stack traces and variable values.

Use Debugging Tools:

Take advantage of the debugging tools provided by your programming language or Integrated Development Environment

(IDE). These tools offer features such as breakpoints, step-by-step execution, variable inspection, and call stack analysis. Familiarize yourself with these tools and learn how to utilize them effectively.

Debugging Techniques:

Apply various debugging techniques such as print statements, logging, and debugging statements to track the flow of your code, inspect variable values, and identify problematic areas. Experiment with different techniques to find the most suitable approach for the given situation.

Write Unit Tests:

Create unit tests that cover different scenarios and validate the behavior of your code. When encountering a bug, start by creating a test case that reproduces the issue. This helps in verifying the fix and ensuring that the bug does not reappear in the future.

Collaborate and Seek Assistance:

Don't hesitate to seek help from colleagues or online communities when encountering challenging bugs. Collaborative debugging can provide fresh perspectives, additional insights, and alternative approaches to finding a solution.

Document the Bug and Fix:

Maintain a record of the bugs you encounter, including their descriptions, steps to reproduce, and the fix implemented. This documentation helps in knowledge sharing, tracking recurring issues, and building a robust codebase.

Test with Minimal Code:

When debugging a complex issue, try to isolate the problem by creating a minimal, reproducible example. Strip away unnecessary code and dependencies to focus solely on the issue at hand. This helps in pinpointing the problem and avoids distractions from unrelated parts of the code.

Check Assumptions:

Double-check your assumptions about how a certain piece of code should work. Ensure that your understanding of the programming language, libraries, and frameworks is accurate. Sometimes, incorrect assumptions can lead to errors that are difficult to spot.

Step Through the Code:

Use step-by-step execution to carefully analyze the flow of your code. Observe the values of variables at each step and compare them with your expectations. This technique can help identify incorrect variable assignments, unexpected loops, or conditions that are not met.

Debug in Different Environments:

If your code behaves differently in different environments (e.g., development vs. production), try to reproduce the issue in various setups. Differences in configurations, dependencies, or data can contribute to bugs. Replicating the environment where the issue occurs can help identify the root cause.

Read the Documentation:

Consult the documentation of the programming language, frameworks, libraries, or APIs you are using. It may contain important information or caveats related to the specific behavior that you are troubleshooting. The documentation can provide insights or even highlight known issues and their solutions.

Use Code Reviews:

Engage in code reviews with your peers. Fresh eyes can spot problems that you may have missed. Code reviews promote knowledge sharing and can help identify issues early on, reducing the likelihood of bugs in the first place.

Take Breaks:

Debugging can be mentally challenging and time-consuming. If you find yourself stuck or getting frustrated, take a break. Stepping away from the code for a while can provide you with a fresh perspective when you return.

Learn from Debugging:

Treat debugging as an opportunity for learning and growth. Each bug encountered is an opportunity to improve your understanding of the codebase, programming concepts, and problem-solving skills. Document the bugs and their solutions to create a knowledge base that can benefit you and your team in the future.

Remember, debugging is a skill that improves with experience. Embrace a systematic and methodical approach, leverage available tools, and be patient and persistent when resolving bugs. By following these best practices, you can enhance your debugging efficiency and produce more reliable software.

Chapter 7: File Handling and Input/Output Operations

Reading and Writing Text Files

Reading and writing text files is a fundamental operation in many programming tasks. Here's an overview of how you can read from and write to text files using common programming languages:

Reading from a Text File:

Open the File:

Open the text file in read mode to access its contents.

```python
file = open("filename.txt", "r")
```

Read the File Contents:

Read the contents of the file using appropriate methods.

In Python:

Read the entire file:

```python
content = file.read()
```

Read a specific number of characters:

```python
content = file.read(100)   # Read 100 characters
```

Read the file line by line:

```python
for line in file:
    print(line)
```

Close the File:

Close the file once you have finished reading its contents.

In Python:

```python
file.close()
```

Writing to a Text File:

Open the File:

Open the text file in write mode to write or overwrite its contents.

In Python:

```python
file = open("filename.txt", "w")
```

Write to the File:

Write the desired text to the file using appropriate methods.

In Python:

Write a single line of text:

```python
file.write("Hello, World!")
```

Write multiple lines of text:

```python
file.write("Line 1\n")
file.write("Line 2\n")
```

Close the File:

Close the file once you have finished writing to it.

In Python:

```python
file.close()
```

It's important to handle file exceptions and errors gracefully, such as file not found or permission issues. Consider using error-handling mechanisms like try-catch blocks or context managers (e.g., with statement in Python) to ensure proper file handling and prevent resource leaks.

Additionally, some programming languages offer higher-level abstractions or libraries that simplify file operations, such as java.nio package in Java or Pathlib module in Python, which provide more convenient ways to read and write text files.

Remember to always follow best practices for file handling, such as closing files after use and handling exceptions appropriately to ensure smooth and efficient file operations.

Working with CSV and JSON Files

Working with CSV and JSON files is a common task in data processing and exchange. Both formats are widely used for storing and manipulating structured data. Here's an overview of how to work with CSV and JSON files in Python:

Working with CSV Files:

Reading CSV Files:

Python provides the csv module for reading and writing CSV files. You can use the csv.reader object to read data from a CSV file.

Here's an example of reading a CSV file:

```python
import csv

with open('data.csv', 'r') as file:
    csv_reader = csv.reader(file)
    for row in csv_reader:
        print(row)
```

Writing CSV Files:

You can use the csv.writer object to write data to a CSV file.

Here's an example of writing data to a CSV file:

```python
import csv

data = [
    ['Name', 'Age', 'Country'],
    ['John', '25', 'USA'],
    ['Alice', '30', 'Canada'],
    ['Bob', '28', 'UK']
]

with open('data.csv', 'w', newline='') as file:
    csv_writer = csv.writer(file)
    csv_writer.writerows(data)
```

Working with CSV Headers:

CSV files often have headers that define the column names. You can access and handle headers separately from the data using the csv.DictReader and csv.DictWriter objects.

Here's an example of working with CSV headers:

```python
import csv

with open('data.csv', 'r') as file:
    csv_reader = csv.DictReader(file)
    for row in csv_reader:
        print(row['Name'], row['Age'], row['Country'])
```

Working with JSON Files:

Reading JSON Files:

Python provides built-in support for working with JSON data through the json module. You can use the json.load function to read data from a JSON file.

Here's an example of reading a JSON file:

```python
import json

with open('data.json', 'r') as file:
    data = json.load(file)
    print(data)
```

Writing JSON Files:

You can use the json.dump function to write data to a JSON file.

Here's an example of writing data to a JSON file:

```python
import json

data = {
    'name': 'John',
    'age': 25,
    'country': 'USA'
}

with open('data.json', 'w') as file:
    json.dump(data, file)
```

Working with JSON Data:

Once the JSON data is loaded into Python, you can access and manipulate it as a dictionary or list, depending on the JSON structure.

Here's an example of accessing JSON data:

```python
import json

with open('data.json', 'r') as file:
    data = json.load(file)
    print(data['name'], data['age'], data['country'])
```

Working with CSV and JSON files allows you to import, export, and process data in different formats. By utilizing the appropriate Python modules (csv and json), you can easily handle structured data and perform various operations on it.

File Manipulation in Python

File manipulation is a fundamental aspect of working with data and storing information. In Python, you can perform various file operations using built-in functions and modules. Here's an overview of file manipulation in Python:

Opening and Closing Files:

You can use the open() function to open a file. It takes two arguments: the file path and the mode (read, write, append, etc.).

After performing the necessary operations, it is important to close the file using the close() method or by utilizing the with statement, which automatically closes the file when the block of code completes.

Here's an example of opening and closing a file:

```python
# Opening a file
file = open('myfile.txt', 'r')

# Performing operations on the file

# Closing the file
file.close()
```

OR

```python
# Opening a file using 'with' statement
with open('myfile.txt', 'r') as file:
    # Performing operations on the file

# File is automatically closed outside the 'with' block
```

Reading File Contents:

To read the contents of a file, you can use the read() method to read the entire file or the readline() method to read a single line at a time.

Here's an example of reading a file:

```python
with open('myfile.txt', 'r') as file:
    content = file.read()  # Read the entire file
    print(content)

    file.seek(0)  # Reset the file pointer

    line = file.readline()  # Read a single line
    print(line)
```

Writing to Files:

To write data to a file, open it in write mode ('w') or append mode ('a'), and use the write() method to write content to the file.

Here's an example of writing to a file:

with open('myfile.txt', 'w') as file:

    file.write("Hello, World!") # Write content to the file

with open('myfile.txt', 'a') as file:

file.write("This is appended content.") # Append content to the file

File Iteration:

You can iterate over the lines of a file using a for loop. Each iteration will provide you with a single line from the file.

Here's an example of iterating over a file:

```python
with open('myfile.txt', 'r') as file:
    for line in file:
        print(line)
```

File Management and Metadata:

Python's os module provides functions for file management and accessing file metadata. You can perform operations like renaming files, deleting files, checking file existence, and more.

Here's an example of file management using the os module:

```python
import os

# Rename a file
os.rename('oldfile.txt', 'newfile.txt')

# Delete a file
os.remove('myfile.txt')

# Check if a file exists
if os.path.exists('myfile.txt'):
    print("File exists.")
```

File manipulation in Python allows you to read, write, and manage files efficiently. Whether you're working with text files, CSV files, JSON files, or any other file format, Python provides the necessary tools and functions to handle file operations effectively. Remember to handle file exceptions and close files appropriately to ensure proper resource management.

Standard Input and Output

Standard input (stdin) and standard output (stdout) are the default channels for input and output in a computer program. In Python, you can interact with stdin and stdout using the built-in input() and print() functions. Here's an overview of standard input and output in Python:

Standard Input (stdin):

Reading User Input:

The input() function is used to read user input from the command line. It prompts the user for input and waits for them to enter a value followed by the Enter key.

The input is returned as a string, so you may need to convert it to the desired data type if necessary.

Here's an example of reading user input:

```python
name = input("Enter your name: ")
age = int(input("Enter your age: "))
```

Standard Output (stdout):

Printing Output:

The print() function is used to display output on the console or terminal. It takes one or more arguments and prints them to the standard output.

By default, print() adds a newline character after the printed content. You can change this behavior by modifying the end parameter.

Here's an example of printing output:

```python
print("Hello, World!")
print("My name is", name)
```

Formatting Output:

The print() function allows you to format output using placeholders or f-strings.

Placeholders: You can use placeholders like %s for strings, %d for integers, %f for floats, and more to format output.

Here's an example using placeholders:

```python
name = "Alice"
age = 25
print("Name: %s, Age: %d" % (name, age))
```

f-strings (formatted strings): Introduced in Python 3.6, f-strings provide a concise and readable way to format strings. You can include variables or expressions within curly braces {} directly in the string.

Here's an example using f-strings:

```python
name = "Alice"
age = 25
print(f"Name: {name}, Age: {age}")
```

Redirecting Output:

You can redirect the standard output to a file instead of the console. This allows you to save the output to a file for later use or analysis.

You can use the > operator to redirect output to a file. For example:

```python
with open('output.txt', 'w') as file:
    print("Hello, World!", file=file)
```

This will write the output to the file 'output.txt' instead of displaying it on the console.

Standard input and output are essential for interacting with the user and displaying results in a Python program. By utilizing the input() and print() functions, you can effectively handle user input, display output, and format your results as needed.

Chapter 8: Introduction to Algorithms and Problem Solving

What is an Algorithm?

An algorithm is a step-by-step procedure or a set of rules for solving a specific problem or accomplishing a particular task. It is a well-defined and finite sequence of instructions that, when followed in a specific order, leads to the desired outcome. Algorithms can be implemented in various programming languages to automate and solve complex problems efficiently.

Here are some key characteristics of algorithms:

Well-defined: Algorithms have precise and unambiguous instructions that can be followed without any ambiguity or confusion. Each step of the algorithm must be clearly defined and understandable.

Finite: Algorithms have a specific start and end point. They must terminate after a finite number of steps. A looping or recursive algorithm should have a termination condition to prevent infinite execution.

Input and Output: Algorithms take input data, operate on it, and produce an output. The input represents the initial problem or data to be processed, and the output represents the solution or the result of the algorithm's execution.

Deterministic: Algorithms are deterministic, meaning that for the same input, they will always produce the same output. The execution of an algorithm should be predictable and reproducible.

Efficiency: Algorithms aim to solve problems efficiently, optimizing for factors such as time complexity (how long it takes to run) and space complexity (how much memory it requires). An efficient algorithm achieves the desired outcome with the fewest necessary steps or resources.

Modularity: Algorithms can be modular, meaning they can be broken down into smaller, more manageable subproblems. By dividing a complex problem into smaller parts, it becomes easier to understand and solve. Modular algorithms promote code reusability and maintainability.

Analysis: Algorithm analysis involves evaluating the performance and efficiency of an algorithm. It helps determine factors such as time complexity, space complexity, and the scalability of an algorithm. By analyzing algorithms, developers can make informed decisions about which algorithm to choose for a particular problem.

Problem-solving Paradigms: Different problem-solving paradigms exist, each with its own set of algorithmic techniques. Common paradigms include brute force, divide and conquer, dynamic programming, greedy algorithms, and backtracking. Understanding these paradigms allows developers to select appropriate algorithms for specific problem domains.

Optimization: Algorithms can be optimized to improve their efficiency. Optimization techniques include reducing redundant computations, employing data structures that provide faster access and manipulation, and using algorithmic optimizations like memoization or pruning. Optimization often involves trade-offs between time complexity, space complexity, and other factors.

Algorithmic Complexity Classes: Algorithms can be classified into complexity classes based on their resource requirements. The most common classification is based on time complexity, such as O(1), O(log n), O(n), O(n log n), O(n^2), and so on. These classes describe how the running time of an algorithm scales with the size of the input.

Algorithm Design Patterns: Similar to software design patterns, algorithm design patterns provide reusable solutions to common algorithmic problems. Design patterns like binary search, merge sort, breadth-first search, and others offer proven strategies for solving specific types of problems efficiently.

Algorithm Libraries and Resources: Numerous algorithm libraries and resources are available that provide pre-implemented algorithms and data structures. These libraries offer efficient and tested implementations of commonly used algorithms, saving developers time and effort. Additionally, online resources, textbooks, and academic research contribute to the ever-expanding knowledge and advancements in algorithm design and analysis.

Understanding algorithms and employing efficient ones is crucial for software development. By selecting and implementing appropriate algorithms, developers can optimize program performance, reduce resource consumption, and deliver robust solutions. Additionally, algorithmic thinking enhances problem-solving skills, enabling developers to approach challenges systematically and creatively.

Understanding Problem Solving Approaches

Problem-solving approaches are systematic strategies used to tackle complex problems and find effective solutions. They provide a structured framework for understanding the problem, identifying potential solutions, and implementing the best course of action. Here are some common problem-solving approaches:

Understand the Problem:

Begin by thoroughly understanding the problem statement or requirements. Break down the problem into smaller components and identify the key objectives and constraints.

Define the Problem:

Clearly define the problem in your own words. This step ensures that you have a precise understanding of what needs to be solved.

Gather Information:

Gather all the relevant information and data related to the problem. This may involve conducting research, consulting documentation or specifications, and seeking input from domain experts.

Analyze the Problem:

Analyze the problem to identify its underlying causes, dependencies, and patterns. Consider the relationships between different variables or factors that contribute to the problem.

Generate Potential Solutions:

Brainstorm and generate a list of potential solutions. Encourage creativity and consider both conventional and unconventional approaches. Avoid evaluating solutions at this stage; focus on generating as many ideas as possible.

Evaluate and Select the Best Solution:

Evaluate each potential solution based on feasibility, effectiveness, efficiency, and other relevant criteria. Compare the pros and cons of each solution and select the one that best aligns with the problem requirements.

Develop an Action Plan:

Create a step-by-step plan to implement the chosen solution. Break down the solution into smaller tasks and determine the resources, time, and dependencies required for each step.

Implement the Solution:

Put your plan into action by executing the steps outlined in the action plan. This may involve writing code, designing a system, conducting experiments, or performing other necessary actions.

Test and Evaluate the Solution:

Verify the solution's effectiveness and evaluate its performance against the problem requirements. Test the solution with various inputs and scenarios to ensure it produces the desired outcome.

Iterate and Refine:

If the solution does not meet the desired outcome or uncover new issues, iterate the problem-solving process. Analyze the feedback and results, refine the solution, and repeat the steps as necessary.

Document and Communicate:

Document the problem-solving process, including the steps taken, decisions made, and the final solution. Communicate the solution and its rationale to stakeholders, clients, or other team members effectively.

Learn from Experience:

Reflect on the problem-solving process and learn from your experience. Identify areas for improvement, apply lessons learned to future problem-solving endeavors, and continuously refine your problem-solving skills.

These problem-solving approaches provide a structured framework for tackling complex problems effectively. Applying these strategies enables you to break down problems, think critically, explore various solutions, and implement the most suitable approach for achieving successful outcomes.

Common Algorithms and Data Structures

Algorithms and data structures are fundamental building blocks in computer science and programming. They provide efficient and effective ways to store, process, and manipulate data. Here are some common algorithms and data structures:

Algorithms:

Sorting Algorithms:

Bubble Sort, Insertion Sort, Selection Sort, Merge Sort, Quick Sort, Heap Sort, Radix Sort, etc. These algorithms arrange a collection of data in a specific order, such as ascending or descending.

Searching Algorithms:

Linear Search, Binary Search, Hashing, etc. These algorithms help locate a specific element within a collection of data.

Graph Algorithms:

Breadth-First Search (BFS), Depth-First Search (DFS), Dijkstra's Algorithm, Bellman-Ford Algorithm, Prim's Algorithm, Kruskal's

Algorithm, etc. These algorithms solve various problems related to graph traversal, shortest paths, minimum spanning trees, and more.

Dynamic Programming:

Dynamic programming involves breaking down a complex problem into smaller overlapping subproblems and solving them iteratively. This technique is used to optimize solutions by avoiding redundant computations.

Greedy Algorithms:

Greedy algorithms make locally optimal choices at each step to achieve the overall optimal solution. Examples include Prim's Algorithm for minimum spanning trees and the Knapsack problem.

Backtracking Algorithms:

Backtracking algorithms explore all possible solutions by incrementally building candidates and backtracking when a solution is found to be invalid. Examples include the N-Queens problem and Sudoku solvers.

String Matching Algorithms:

String matching algorithms efficiently search for patterns within strings. Examples include the Knuth-Morris-Pratt (KMP) algorithm and the Boyer-Moore algorithm.

Data Structures:

Arrays:

Arrays are a fundamental data structure that store a fixed-size sequence of elements of the same data type. They provide efficient random access but have a fixed size.

Linked Lists:

Linked lists are dynamic data structures composed of nodes, each containing data and a reference to the next node. They allow for efficient insertion and deletion at any position.

Stacks:

Stacks are Last-In, First-Out (LIFO) data structures where elements are added and removed from the top. They are commonly used in function calls, expression evaluation, and undo operations.

Queues:

Queues are First-In, First-Out (FIFO) data structures where elements are added at the rear and removed from the front. They are used in scheduling, resource allocation, and breadth-first search.

Trees:

Trees are hierarchical data structures with nodes connected by edges. Examples include Binary Trees, Binary Search Trees (BSTs), AVL Trees, and Red-Black Trees. Trees are widely used for efficient searching, sorting, and organizing hierarchical relationships.

Graphs:

Graphs are a collection of nodes (vertices) connected by edges. They represent various relationships and are used for modeling networks, social connections, and more. Graphs can be directed or undirected, and they support various algorithms for traversal and analysis.

Hash Tables:

Hash tables, also known as hash maps, are data structures that use a hash function to map keys to values. They provide efficient lookup, insertion, and deletion operations. Hash tables are often used for implementing dictionaries or associative arrays.

These are just a few examples of common algorithms and data structures. Understanding and implementing these algorithms and data structures enable efficient problem-solving, data manipulation, and optimization in software development and computer science. It's important to choose the appropriate algorithm and data structure based on the problem at hand and the desired efficiency and functionality.

Algorithm Design Techniques

Algorithm design techniques provide systematic approaches to solving problems and developing efficient algorithms. These techniques help break down complex problems, analyze their characteristics, and devise effective solutions. Here are some common algorithm design techniques:

Divide and Conquer:

Divide and Conquer involves breaking a problem into smaller subproblems, solving them independently, and combining their solutions to obtain the final result. This technique is often used in sorting algorithms (e.g., Merge Sort), searching algorithms (e.g., Binary Search), and many other problem domains.

Greedy Algorithms:

Greedy algorithms make locally optimal choices at each step with the hope of finding a globally optimal solution. They prioritize immediate gains without considering the entire problem space. Greedy algorithms are suitable for problems with optimal substructure and the greedy-choice property. Examples include

Dijkstra's Algorithm for finding the shortest path and the Knapsack problem.

Dynamic Programming:

Dynamic programming breaks a problem into overlapping subproblems and solves them recursively, storing the solutions to avoid redundant computations. It is particularly useful when the problem exhibits optimal substructure, meaning the optimal solution can be built from optimal solutions to subproblems. Dynamic programming is applied in problems like the Fibonacci series, the 0/1 Knapsack problem, and the Longest Common Subsequence problem.

Backtracking:

Backtracking involves systematically exploring all possible solutions by incrementally building a solution candidate and backtracking when it is determined to be invalid. It is used when the problem space is large and exhaustive search is required. Backtracking is employed in problems like the N-Queens problem, Sudoku solvers, and generating permutations or combinations.

Brute Force:

Brute force involves trying all possible solutions exhaustively. Although it may not be the most efficient technique, it can be applicable for small problem sizes or when other techniques are not feasible. Brute force is used when the problem space is small enough to iterate through all possibilities, such as in simple search problems.

Randomized Algorithms:

Randomized algorithms introduce randomness in their execution to improve efficiency or provide probabilistic guarantees. These algorithms leverage the power of randomization to solve problems more efficiently than deterministic approaches. Examples include randomized sorting algorithms like QuickSort and randomized approximation algorithms like Monte Carlo algorithms.

Heuristic Algorithms:

Heuristic algorithms provide approximate solutions to complex problems within a reasonable amount of time. They use rules of thumb or domain-specific knowledge to make informed decisions. Heuristic algorithms sacrifice optimality for efficiency. Examples include the Traveling Salesman Problem using heuristics like the Nearest Neighbor algorithm or the Ant Colony Optimization algorithm.

Branch and Bound:

Branch and Bound is a method used to solve optimization problems by systematically exploring the search space and pruning branches that are unlikely to lead to an optimal solution. It divides the problem into smaller subproblems, creates a search tree, and uses upper and lower bounds to determine which branches to explore and which to discard. Branch and Bound is commonly employed in problems like the Traveling Salesman Problem and the Knapsack Problem.

Reduction:

Reduction is a technique used to solve a problem by transforming it into a different, often simpler problem. If the original problem is difficult to solve, reduction allows us to map it to a known problem for which efficient algorithms already exist. This technique leverages the concept that if problem A can be reduced to problem B, and we have an algorithm for solving problem B, we can use it to solve problem A.

Approximation Algorithms:

Approximation algorithms aim to find near-optimal solutions for hard optimization problems when finding the exact optimal solution is computationally infeasible. These algorithms trade off optimality for efficiency and provide solutions that are guaranteed to be within a certain factor of the optimal solution. Approximation algorithms are widely used in graph theory, scheduling, and facility location problems.

Randomized Algorithms:

Randomized algorithms introduce randomness in their execution to improve efficiency or provide probabilistic guarantees. They leverage the power of randomization to solve problems more efficiently than deterministic approaches. Randomized algorithms are particularly useful in situations where exact solutions are not required or when it is difficult to find deterministic solutions with acceptable time complexity.

Parallel and Distributed Algorithms:

Parallel and distributed algorithms leverage multiple computational resources, such as multiple processors or networked systems, to solve problems more efficiently. These algorithms divide the problem into subproblems that can be solved concurrently, taking advantage of parallel processing and distributed computing architectures. Parallel and distributed algorithms are used in various domains, including data analysis, scientific simulations, and large-scale optimization.

Online Algorithms:

Online algorithms are designed to handle problems where inputs arrive in a sequential manner, and decisions must be made immediately without knowledge of future inputs. These algorithms make decisions based on the available information at each step, adapting to changing conditions. Online algorithms are commonly used in resource allocation, scheduling, and network optimization problems.

Metaheuristic Algorithms:

Metaheuristic algorithms are high-level strategies that guide the exploration of solution spaces to find near-optimal solutions for complex optimization problems. They are often inspired by natural processes like evolution, swarm behavior, or simulated annealing. Metaheuristic algorithms, such as Genetic Algorithms, Particle Swarm Optimization, and Simulated Annealing, can effectively handle problems where other techniques fail to provide efficient solutions.

These algorithm design techniques offer different strategies for approaching problem-solving and algorithm development. Understanding these techniques allows you to choose the most appropriate approach for a given problem, leading to efficient and effective solutions. It's important to consider the problem characteristics, constraints, and requirements when selecting the appropriate algorithm design technique.

Chapter 9: Introduction to Web Development

Basics of HTML

HTML (Hypertext Markup Language) is a standard markup language used for creating the structure and content of web pages. It uses various tags and elements to define the different parts of a web page. Here are some basics of HTML:

HTML Document Structure:

An HTML document begins with the <!DOCTYPE html> declaration, which specifies the HTML version being used (HTML5 in this case).

The document's root element is <html>, and it contains two main sections: <head> and <body>.

The <head> section contains meta information, such as the page title, character encoding, and linked stylesheets or scripts.

The <body> section contains the visible content of the web page.

HTML Tags and Elements:

HTML uses tags to define elements and structure the content of a web page.

Tags are enclosed within angle brackets (< and >), and most tags come in pairs: an opening tag and a closing tag.

Opening tags contain the element's name, while closing tags have a forward slash (/) before the element's name.

For example, <h1> is an opening tag for a heading, and </h1> is a closing tag for the same heading element.

Common HTML Elements:

<h1> to <h6>: Heading elements for different levels of headings.

<p>: Paragraph element for text content.

<a>: Anchor element for creating hyperlinks.

<img>: Image element for displaying images.

<ul>: Unordered list element.

<ol>: Ordered list element.

<li>: List item element.

<table>: Table element for creating tables.

<form>: Form element for gathering user input.

<input>: Input element for various form controls like text fields, checkboxes, radio buttons, etc.

Attributes:

HTML elements can have attributes that provide additional information or modify the behavior of the element.

Attributes are specified within the opening tag of an element.

Examples of attributes include src for specifying the source of an image or href for specifying the URL of a hyperlink.

Nesting and Hierarchical Structure:

HTML elements can be nested inside other elements to create a hierarchical structure.

For example, a paragraph element (<p>) can contain a link element (<a>), and the link element can contain text or other elements.

Semantic HTML:

Semantic HTML aims to give meaning to the structure and content of a web page.

It uses specific elements to convey the intended purpose or meaning of different parts of the page, such as <header>, <nav>, <article>, <footer>, etc.

Using semantic elements helps improve accessibility, search engine optimization, and overall code readability.

HTML provides the foundation for creating web pages and defining their structure and content. By using the various tags, elements, and attributes, you can create well-structured web documents. As you progress, you can learn more about styling with CSS, adding interactivity with JavaScript, and exploring advanced HTML features to enhance the functionality and visual appeal of your web pages.

CSS Fundamentals

CSS (Cascading Style Sheets) is a styling language used to describe the presentation and appearance of HTML documents. It allows you to control the layout, colors, fonts, and other visual aspects of web pages. Here are some CSS fundamentals to get you started:

CSS Syntax:

CSS rules consist of selectors and declarations. Selectors target HTML elements, and declarations specify the styling properties and values.

The basic syntax for a CSS rule is: selector { property: value; }.

Multiple declarations can be included within a rule, separated by semicolons.

CSS Selectors:

CSS selectors specify which HTML elements to target and style.

Some commonly used selectors include:

Element selector: Targets all instances of a specific HTML element. Example: p { color: blue; }

Class selector: Targets elements with a specific class attribute. Example: .my-class { font-weight: bold; }

ID selector: Targets a specific element with a unique ID attribute. Example: #my-id { background-color: yellow; }

Attribute selector: Targets elements with a specific attribute value. Example: input[type="text"] { border: 1px solid gray; }

Pseudo-class selector: Targets elements in specific states or conditions. Example: a:hover { text-decoration: underline; }

CSS Properties and Values:

CSS properties define the styling aspects, and values specify how those properties should be applied.

Common CSS properties include color, font-size, margin, padding, background-color, border, width, height, text-align, display, and many more.

Property values can be in different units, such as pixels (px), percentages (%), em units (em), and more.

CSS Box Model:

The CSS box model describes how elements are laid out and how their dimensions are calculated.

It consists of content, padding, border, and margin.

The width and height of an element are calculated by adding the content, padding, and border, but excluding the margin.

CSS Cascading and Specificity:

CSS follows a cascading order, where multiple style rules can target the same element, and their styles are applied based on specificity and order.

Specificity is a value that determines which style rule takes precedence over others.

Inline styles have the highest specificity, followed by IDs, classes, and element selectors.

CSS Inheritance:

CSS properties can be inherited from parent elements to their child elements.

Some properties, like color and font-family, are inherited by default, while others, like padding and border, are not.

CSS Media Queries:

Media queries allow you to apply different styles based on specific conditions, such as screen size, device orientation, or print media.

By using media queries, you can create responsive designs that adapt to different devices and screen sizes.

CSS Box Layout and Flexbox:

CSS provides different layout options, including traditional box layout (display: block and display: inline-block) and Flexbox (display: flex and display: inline-flex).

Flexbox is a powerful layout model that enables flexible and responsive designs by arranging elements in a flexible row or column-based structure.

These are the fundamental concepts of CSS. By understanding and applying these principles, you can style and customize the appearance of your web pages, create responsive layouts, and enhance the overall user experience. As you explore further, you can dive into advanced CSS features, animations, transitions, and CSS frameworks to streamline your styling workflow.

JavaScript Essentials

JavaScript is a powerful programming language primarily used for developing interactive web pages and web applications. It enables dynamic behavior, manipulation of webpage elements, and interaction with users. Here are some JavaScript essentials to get you started:

Variables and Data Types:

Variables are used to store and manipulate data in JavaScript. They are declared using the var, let, or const keywords.

JavaScript has several built-in data types, including numbers, strings, booleans, objects, arrays, and null/undefined.

Operators and Expressions:

JavaScript provides various operators for performing arithmetic, comparison, logical, and assignment operations.

Expressions combine variables, values, and operators to produce a resulting value.

Control Flow:

JavaScript uses control flow statements such as if...else, switch, for, while, and do...while to control the execution of code based on conditions.

Functions:

Functions are reusable blocks of code that perform specific tasks. They help organize code, improve modularity, and promote code reuse.

Functions can take parameters as inputs and return values as outputs.

Objects:

Objects in JavaScript are collections of properties and methods.

Properties are variables that hold values, while methods are functions associated with objects.

Objects can be created using object literals or constructor functions.

Arrays:

Arrays in JavaScript are used to store multiple values in a single variable.

They are ordered, indexed collections of elements, and can contain values of different data types.

Arrays provide built-in methods for manipulating and accessing their elements.

DOM Manipulation:

The Document Object Model (DOM) represents the structure of an HTML document and allows JavaScript to access and manipulate its elements.

JavaScript can modify HTML elements, change their styles, add or remove elements, and handle user interactions.

Events:

JavaScript can respond to user interactions and other events on a webpage, such as clicks, keypresses, mouse movements, and form submissions.

Event listeners can be added to HTML elements to execute JavaScript code when specific events occur.

Error Handling:

JavaScript provides mechanisms to handle and manage errors through try-catch statements.

Try blocks contain the code that might generate an error, and catch blocks handle the errors and provide alternative actions.

Asynchronous Programming:

JavaScript supports asynchronous programming using callbacks, promises, and async/await.

Asynchronous operations, such as fetching data from a server or waiting for a user input, can be handled without blocking the execution of other code.

Libraries and Frameworks:

JavaScript has a vast ecosystem of libraries and frameworks that extend its capabilities and simplify common tasks.

Popular libraries include jQuery, React.js, Vue.js, and AngularJS, while frameworks like Node.js enable server-side JavaScript development.

JavaScript is a versatile language with a wide range of applications. By mastering these essentials, you can create interactive web pages, handle user interactions, manipulate webpage elements, and build complex web applications. Continuous learning and exploration of JavaScript's features and libraries will further enhance your skills and empower you to create dynamic and engaging web experiences.

Building Simple Web Applications

Building simple web applications involves combining HTML, CSS, and JavaScript to create interactive and dynamic functionality. Here's a step-by-step guide to get you started:

Plan and Design:

Define the purpose and functionality of your web application.

Sketch a rough layout of the user interface to visualize the structure and components.

Set up the Project:

Create a new project folder on your computer.

Create an HTML file (index.html) and a CSS file (styles.css) in the project folder.

Link the CSS file to the HTML file using the <link> tag within the <head> section.

Structure the HTML:

Design the HTML structure based on your project requirements.

Use HTML tags to create the necessary elements such as headings, paragraphs, forms, buttons, and div containers.

Assign IDs or classes to elements for easy selection and manipulation with CSS and JavaScript.

Style with CSS:

Add styles to your HTML elements using CSS rules.

Select elements using IDs, classes, or element selectors and apply styles using property-value pairs.

Experiment with different font styles, colors, backgrounds, margins, padding, and layout techniques to achieve your desired design.

Add Interactivity with JavaScript:

Enhance your web application by adding JavaScript functionality.

Use event listeners to respond to user interactions like button clicks or form submissions.

Access HTML elements using document.getElementById() or document.querySelector() and manipulate them based on user actions.

Perform calculations, validate form inputs, show/hide elements, or update content dynamically using JavaScript.

Test and Debug:

Test your web application on different browsers and devices to ensure compatibility and responsiveness.

Use browser developer tools to inspect elements, debug JavaScript code, and fix any issues.

Test user interactions and validate that the application behaves as expected.

Deploy:

Host your web application on a web server or deploy it to a hosting platform to make it accessible on the internet.

Ensure all necessary files (HTML, CSS, JavaScript) are uploaded correctly.

Share the URL with others to showcase your web application.

Iterate and Refine:

Gather feedback from users and iterate on your design and functionality based on their input.

Continuously improve and refine your web application by adding new features or addressing any usability issues.

As you gain more experience, you can explore advanced techniques, frameworks, and libraries to build more complex web applications. Remember to practice good coding practices, maintain code readability, and stay updated with the latest web development trends.

Chapter 10: Version Control with Git

Introduction to Version Control

Version control is a system that allows you to track changes to files and collaborate with others on a project. It helps manage the evolution of files, keeps a history of modifications, and enables teams to work on the same codebase efficiently. One popular version control system is Git. Here's an introduction to version control using Git:

Install Git:

Start by installing Git on your computer. Git provides an easy-to-use command-line interface and can be downloaded from the official website (https://git-scm.com) or installed using package managers.

Initialize a Repository:

Create a new folder for your project and navigate to it using the command line.

Initialize a Git repository in that folder by running the command: git init.

This initializes a new Git repository, which will track changes to files within that folder.

Track Changes:

Git tracks changes to files within the repository.

Add files to the repository using the command: git add filename or git add . to add all files in the current directory.

Once added, files are staged and ready to be committed.

Commit Changes:

Committing captures a snapshot of the changes made to the files at a specific point in time.

Commit changes using the command: git commit -m "Commit message".

The commit message should describe the changes made in the commit.

View History:

Git maintains a history of commits, allowing you to view the changes made over time.

Use the command: git log to see the commit history, including commit IDs, authors, dates, and commit messages.

Branching and Merging:

Branching allows you to create separate lines of development within the same repository.

Create a new branch using the command: git branch branchname.

Switch to a branch using: git checkout branchname.

Merging combines changes from one branch into another using: git merge branchname.

Collaborate with Remote Repositories:

Git enables collaboration by allowing you to work with remote repositories.

Create a remote repository on a hosting platform like GitHub or GitLab.

Connect your local repository to the remote repository using: git remote add origin <remote repository URL>.

Push your local changes to the remote repository using: git push origin branchname.

Fetch and merge changes from the remote repository using: git fetch origin followed by git merge origin/branchname.

Resolving Conflicts:

When merging or pulling changes, conflicts may arise if the same file was modified in different ways.

Git provides tools to help resolve conflicts manually by editing the conflicting files.

Use git status to identify conflicted files and then edit them to resolve conflicts.

Commit the resolved changes to finalize the merge or pull.

Version control with Git offers numerous benefits, such as easy collaboration, history tracking, code organization, and the ability to revert changes if necessary. It is a crucial tool for developers working on projects of any scale, from small personal projects to large-scale team collaborations.

Setting Up Git

To set up Git on your computer, follow these steps:

Download and Install Git:

Visit the official Git website (https://git-scm.com) and download the appropriate version for your operating system.

Run the installer and follow the prompts to complete the installation process.

Configure Git:

Open a terminal or command prompt.

Set your name by running the command: git config --global user.name "Your Name".

Set your email address by running the command: git config --global user.email "youremail@example.com".

These configurations will be associated with your Git commits.

Check Git Version:

To verify that Git is installed correctly, run the command: git --version.

It should display the Git version installed on your computer.

Optional Configuration:

You can configure additional settings, such as your preferred text editor and line-ending settings.

To set a default text editor, use the command: git config --global core.editor "your-editor". Replace "your-editor" with the command or path to your preferred text editor.

To handle line-ending conversions, use the command: git config --global core.autocrlf true for Windows or git config --global core.autocrlf input for macOS and Linux.

Generate SSH Key (Optional):

If you plan to use Git with remote repositories that require SSH authentication, you can generate an SSH key.

Run the command: ssh-keygen -t rsa -b 4096 -C "your-email@example.com".

Follow the prompts to choose a location for the key and set a passphrase if desired.

Add the SSH key to your remote repository account as per their documentation.

You have now set up Git on your computer. You can start using Git by creating a new repository or cloning an existing one. To create a new repository, navigate to the desired project directory, and run the command: git init. To clone an existing repository, use the command: git clone <repository-url>.

Remember to refer to the Git documentation or online resources for more advanced Git usage and to explore the various commands and workflows available.

Basic Git Commands

Here are some basic Git commands to get you started:

git init:

Initializes a new Git repository in the current directory. It creates a hidden .git folder that stores the repository's data.

git clone <repository-url>:

Clones an existing Git repository from a remote location to your local machine.

Replace <repository-url> with the URL of the repository you want to clone.

git status:

Shows the current state of the repository.

It displays which files are modified, which files are staged (added to be committed), and which files are untracked.

git add <file>:

Adds a file to the staging area, preparing it for the next commit.

Replace <file> with the name of the file you want to add.

Use git add . to add all modified and untracked files in the current directory.

git commit -m "Commit message":

Records the changes made to the files in the repository.

The -m flag allows you to provide a short and descriptive commit message within double quotes.

git push:

Pushes your local commits to a remote repository.

Use git push origin <branch-name> to push the commits to a specific branch on the remote repository.

git pull:

Fetches and merges changes from a remote repository to your local repository.

It updates your local repository with the latest changes made by others.

Use git pull origin <branch-name> to pull changes from a specific branch.

git branch:

Lists all the branches in the repository.

The current branch is indicated with an asterisk.

Use git branch <branch-name> to create a new branch.

Use git branch -d <branch-name> to delete a branch.

git checkout <branch-name>:

Switches to a different branch in the repository.

Replace <branch-name> with the name of the branch you want to switch to.

git merge <branch-name>:

Merges changes from a different branch into the current branch.

Use git merge <branch-name> to merge the changes from <branch-name> into the current branch.

git log:

Displays a history of commits in the repository.

It shows the commit hash, author, date, and commit message for each commit.

These are some of the most commonly used Git commands to manage your repository's history, collaborate with others, and maintain different branches. As you become more comfortable with Git, you can explore additional commands and workflows to enhance your version control experience.

Collaborating with Others Using Git

Collaborating with others using Git involves sharing code repositories, tracking changes, and managing contributions from multiple team members. Here's an overview of the key steps and Git commands involved in collaborative workflows:

Forking a Repository:

Forking a repository creates a personal copy of someone else's repository on a remote Git hosting platform like GitHub or GitLab.

Use the "Fork" button on the hosting platform to create your forked repository.

Cloning a Repository:

Clone the forked repository to your local machine using the git clone command.

Copy the repository's URL from the hosting platform and run: git clone <repository-url> in the command line.

This creates a local copy of the repository that you can work with.

Adding an Upstream Remote:

To keep your forked repository in sync with the original repository, you need to add an upstream remote.

Run: git remote add upstream <original-repo-url> to add the upstream remote.

This allows you to fetch and merge changes from the original repository into your local repository.

Creating and Switching Branches:

Create a new branch to work on a specific feature or issue using the git branch command.

Run: git branch <branch-name> to create a new branch.

Switch to the new branch using: git checkout <branch-name>.

Making and Committing Changes:

Make changes to the files in your local repository.

Use git add to stage the changes, and then git commit to commit them with a descriptive message.

Repeat this process as you make changes to different files or work on different features.

Pushing Changes to Your Forked Repository:

Push your local branch and commits to your forked repository using git push origin <branch-name>.

This makes your changes available in your forked repository.

Creating a Pull Request:

Once you have pushed your changes to your forked repository, you can create a pull request to propose merging your changes into the original repository.

Go to the original repository on the hosting platform and click on the "New Pull Request" button.

Select your branch from the forked repository and provide a descriptive title and description for the pull request.

Review the changes, add any additional comments, and submit the pull request.

Reviewing and Merging Pull Requests:

Other team members or maintainers of the original repository can review your pull request, provide feedback, and request changes if needed.

Once the changes are approved, the maintainers can merge the pull request, integrating your changes into the original repository.

Syncing with Upstream Changes:

Regularly sync your forked repository with the original repository to incorporate any new changes made by others.

Fetch the upstream changes using git fetch upstream and then merge them into your local branch using git merge upstream/main.

This ensures that your local repository stays up to date with the latest changes.

Collaborating with others using Git involves a combination of local development, remote repository management, and effective communication through pull requests and code reviews. By following these steps and using the appropriate Git commands, you can work seamlessly with your team and contribute to shared code repositories.

Chapter 11: Testing and Debugging Your Code

Importance of Testing

Testing is a critical aspect of software development that ensures the quality, reliability, and performance of a software system. It involves systematically verifying and validating the behavior and functionality of the software to identify defects, errors, and potential issues. Here are some key reasons why testing is important in software development:

Detecting and Preventing Bugs:

Testing helps identify bugs, errors, and defects in software before it is deployed or released to users. By detecting these issues early in the development process, they can be addressed and fixed promptly, reducing the risk of encountering them in production.

Ensuring Software Functionality:

Testing ensures that software functions as intended and meets the specified requirements. It verifies that the system performs the expected operations and produces the correct results.

Improving Software Quality:

Testing helps improve the quality of software by identifying and resolving issues that could impact user experience, performance, or security. By uncovering and fixing these issues, software quality is enhanced, leading to a better user experience and higher customer satisfaction.

Enhancing User Confidence:

Thorough testing instills confidence in users, as they have assurance that the software has been tested and verified for functionality and reliability. It establishes trust and credibility in the software, leading to increased user adoption and customer loyalty.

Validating System Performance:

Testing evaluates the performance of the software under different scenarios, load conditions, and user interactions. It helps identify performance bottlenecks, scalability issues, and resource limitations. This allows developers to optimize the software's performance and ensure it can handle expected workloads.

Supporting Maintenance and Upgrades:

Testing plays a crucial role in supporting software maintenance and upgrades. When new features or updates are introduced, testing ensures that existing functionality remains intact and that new changes do not introduce regressions or conflicts with the existing codebase.

Ensuring Compatibility:

Testing ensures that software works seamlessly across different platforms, devices, and configurations. It validates compatibility with various operating systems, web browsers, and hardware to provide a consistent user experience across different environments.

Reducing Development Costs:

Detecting and fixing defects early in the development process helps reduce overall development costs. By catching issues early, developers spend less time and effort on debugging and troubleshooting, leading to increased efficiency and productivity.

Regulatory and Compliance Requirements:

For software in regulated industries, testing is essential to meet regulatory and compliance requirements. Testing ensures that the software adheres to industry standards, security protocols, privacy regulations, and accessibility guidelines.

Continuous Improvement:

Testing is an iterative process that helps identify areas for improvement. By analyzing test results and feedback, developers can refine their code, enhance functionality, and optimize performance in subsequent iterations.

In summary, testing is crucial in software development to identify defects, improve quality, validate functionality, enhance performance, and ensure user satisfaction. It is an ongoing process that should be integrated throughout the development lifecycle, from initial development to maintenance and upgrades. By investing in thorough testing practices, organizations can deliver reliable, high-quality software that meets user expectations and drives business success.

Types of Testing

There are various types of testing techniques used in software development to verify and validate different aspects of the software. Here are some commonly used types of testing:

Unit Testing:

Unit testing focuses on testing individual units or components of the software in isolation. It verifies that each unit functions correctly as per its design and meets its specific requirements.

Unit tests are typically written by developers and executed frequently to catch bugs and errors early in the development process.

Integration Testing:

Integration testing verifies the interactions and interfaces between different components or modules of the software. It ensures that these components work together correctly and exchange data as intended.

Integration tests identify issues that may arise from the integration of different units or subsystems and help ensure the smooth functioning of the software as a whole.

System Testing:

System testing is conducted on the complete and integrated software system to evaluate its compliance with specified requirements.

It tests the system's behavior, functionality, performance, and reliability under various scenarios, validating that it meets the desired expectations.

Acceptance Testing:

Acceptance testing involves evaluating the software's compliance with user requirements and ensuring that it satisfies the users' needs.

It is typically performed by end users or stakeholders to determine if the software is acceptable and ready for deployment.

Acceptance testing can include User Acceptance Testing (UAT) and Business Acceptance Testing (BAT).

Performance Testing:

Performance testing evaluates the responsiveness, scalability, and stability of the software under different load conditions and usage scenarios.

It measures and analyzes factors such as response time, throughput, resource usage, and reliability to ensure the software performs optimally.

Security Testing:

Security testing focuses on identifying vulnerabilities, weaknesses, and potential risks in the software's security mechanisms.

It involves assessing the system's ability to protect data, prevent unauthorized access, and ensure compliance with security standards.

Regression Testing:

Regression testing ensures that recent changes or updates to the software do not introduce new defects or cause existing functionality to fail.

It retests previously working features to validate their continued functionality in the presence of new changes.

Usability Testing:

Usability testing evaluates the software's user-friendliness, ease of use, and overall user experience.

It involves observing users as they interact with the software to identify areas of confusion, inefficiency, or difficulties in navigation or task completion.

Exploratory Testing:

Exploratory testing is an unscripted testing approach where testers explore the software without predefined test cases.

Testers use their knowledge, experience, and intuition to uncover defects, assess the software's behavior, and provide valuable feedback.

Continuous Integration and Continuous Testing:

Continuous Integration (CI) and Continuous Testing (CT) are practices that involve automatically building, testing, and validating the software with each code change.

CI/CT pipelines ensure that any changes introduced to the codebase are validated through automated tests, allowing developers to catch issues early and maintain code quality.

These are just a few examples of testing types commonly used in software development. Each type serves a specific purpose and addresses different aspects of software quality and functionality. Depending on the nature of the software and its requirements, multiple testing types may be employed to ensure comprehensive testing coverage.

Writing Test Cases

Writing effective test cases is crucial for thorough testing and ensuring software quality. Here are some steps to help you write test cases:

Identify Test Scenarios:

Start by analyzing the requirements, user stories, or specifications to identify the different scenarios and functionalities that need to be tested.

Break down the software into smaller components or features, and consider the various inputs, actions, and expected outcomes for each.

Define Test Objectives:

Clearly define the objectives of each test case. What specific behavior or functionality are you testing? What is the desired outcome or result?

Write Clear and Concise Test Case Titles:

Create a descriptive and concise title for each test case that reflects the specific scenario or functionality being tested.

A good test case title should provide a clear understanding of what is being tested.

Specify Preconditions:

Document any necessary preconditions, such as specific system configurations, data setup, or prerequisite actions that need to be performed before executing the test case.

Describe Test Steps:

Outline the specific steps to be followed to execute the test case.

Include the necessary inputs, actions, or interactions with the software being tested.

Include Expected Results:

Clearly define the expected results or outcomes for each test case.

Specify what the software should do or display in response to the inputs and actions mentioned in the test steps.

Add Additional Details and Data:

Provide any additional details or information that may be necessary to execute the test case effectively.

This may include sample data, test environment specifications, or specific configurations.

Consider Positive and Negative Scenarios:

Test cases should cover both positive and negative scenarios to ensure comprehensive testing.

Positive scenarios verify that the software functions as intended, while negative scenarios test how the software handles invalid inputs, error conditions, or unexpected situations.

Make Test Cases Independent and Reusable:

Each test case should be independent of others, meaning they can be executed individually without dependencies on previous test cases.

Avoid creating test cases that rely on the execution or outcomes of other test cases.

Reusable test cases can be executed in different testing cycles or scenarios to validate specific functionality.

Review and Validate Test Cases:

Conduct a thorough review of the test cases to ensure they are accurate, complete, and meet the testing objectives.

Validate the test cases against the requirements or specifications to confirm that they cover all the necessary scenarios.

Maintain Test Case Documentation:

Organize and maintain a central repository or test management system to store and manage your test cases.

Update the test cases as needed when requirements or functionality change, ensuring that the documentation remains up to date.

Writing effective test cases requires attention to detail, clarity, and a deep understanding of the software's behavior. By following these steps and best practices, you can create comprehensive test cases that help ensure thorough testing and the delivery of high-quality software.

Debugging Techniques and Tools

Debugging is the process of identifying and resolving issues or bugs in software code. It involves investigating the cause of unexpected behavior, errors, or crashes in order to fix them. Here are some debugging techniques and tools that can help in the process:

Print Statements:

One of the simplest and most effective debugging techniques is to use print statements in the code to output specific values or messages at various points.

By strategically placing print statements, you can trace the flow of execution and identify the values of variables or the sequence of events leading to an issue.

Debuggers:

Debuggers are powerful tools that allow you to step through code, set breakpoints, and inspect variables at runtime.

Integrated Development Environments (IDEs) often have built-in debuggers that provide features like stepping through code line by line, examining variable values, and analyzing call stacks.

Common debuggers for different programming languages include GDB (GNU Debugger), PyCharm Debugger, Visual Studio Debugger, and Xcode Debugger.

Breakpoints:

Breakpoints are markers in the code that pause the execution at specific lines or functions, allowing you to examine the program state at that point.

By setting breakpoints strategically, you can investigate the values of variables and the flow of execution to identify the cause of issues.

Logging:

Logging involves using specialized logging frameworks or libraries to capture and record events, error messages, and other relevant information during program execution.

Logging statements can be strategically placed to track the flow of execution and gather valuable insights about the program's behavior.

Log files provide a detailed record that can be analyzed to pinpoint the source of issues.

Error Messages and Stack Traces:

When an error or exception occurs, error messages and stack traces are valuable sources of information for debugging.

Error messages often provide clues about what went wrong, while stack traces show the sequence of function calls leading to the error.

Analyzing error messages and stack traces can help identify the specific code segments or functions causing the issue.

Code Review and Pair Programming:

Collaborative techniques like code review and pair programming involve having another developer review your code or work with you in real-time.

Fresh eyes and a different perspective can often help spot issues or suggest alternative approaches.

Explaining your code to someone else can also lead to a better understanding of the problem and potential solutions.

Automated Testing:

Automated tests can help identify and isolate issues by running specific test cases that reproduce the problem.

By systematically testing different parts of the codebase, you can identify when and where issues occur and narrow down the root cause.

Online Communities and Forums:

Online communities and forums dedicated to specific programming languages or frameworks can be excellent resources for seeking help and advice.

Posting a detailed description of the issue, code snippets, and error messages can often lead to suggestions and insights from experienced developers.

Remember, debugging can be a process of trial and error, and different techniques may be more effective in different situations. The key is to be systematic, patient, and methodical in your approach.

Chapter 12: Introduction to Data Science and Analysis

What is Data Science?

Data science is an interdisciplinary field that combines scientific methods, processes, algorithms, and systems to extract insights and knowledge from structured and unstructured data. It involves collecting, organizing, analyzing, and interpreting vast amounts of data to uncover patterns, trends, and relationships that can inform decision-making and drive business outcomes.

Key components of data science include:

Data Collection and Storage:

Data scientists gather and acquire data from various sources, such as databases, APIs, websites, sensors, and social media platforms.

They ensure the data is properly stored and organized in databases or data warehouses for efficient analysis.

Data Cleaning and Preprocessing:

Raw data is often messy, incomplete, or inconsistent. Data scientists clean and preprocess the data to remove errors, handle missing values, and standardize formats.

They may also perform transformations, normalization, and feature engineering to prepare the data for analysis.

Exploratory Data Analysis (EDA):

EDA involves visually exploring and summarizing the data to understand its characteristics, detect patterns, outliers, and relationships between variables.

Data visualization techniques and statistical methods are used to gain insights and formulate hypotheses.

Machine Learning:

Machine learning is a subset of data science that focuses on building models and algorithms that can learn from data and make predictions or decisions.

Data scientists apply various machine learning techniques, such as supervised learning, unsupervised learning, and reinforcement learning, to solve specific problems.

Statistical Analysis:

Statistical analysis involves applying statistical methods and techniques to draw conclusions, make inferences, and validate hypotheses from data.

Data scientists use statistical modeling, hypothesis testing, and regression analysis to understand relationships, make predictions, and quantify uncertainties.

Data Visualization:

Data visualization is a crucial aspect of data science, as it helps present complex data in a visual format that is easily understandable and interpretable.

Data scientists use charts, graphs, and interactive dashboards to communicate findings, trends, and insights to stakeholders.

Big Data Technologies:

Data science often deals with large volumes of data, requiring the use of big data technologies like Apache Hadoop, Apache Spark, and distributed computing frameworks to process and analyze data efficiently.

Domain Knowledge:

Data scientists possess domain knowledge and expertise in specific industries or fields to understand the context of the data, ask relevant questions, and provide meaningful insights.

They collaborate with domain experts, stakeholders, and decision-makers to translate data insights into actionable strategies.

Data science has applications in various industries and domains, including finance, healthcare, marketing, e-commerce, manufacturing, and more. It empowers organizations to make data-driven decisions, optimize processes, enhance customer experiences, and gain a competitive edge. Data scientists play a crucial role in extracting valuable insights from data and driving innovation through data-driven strategies and solutions.

Data Manipulation with Python

Data manipulation is a fundamental task in data science, and Python provides powerful libraries and tools for handling and manipulating data effectively. Here are some key libraries and techniques for data manipulation with Python:

NumPy:

NumPy is a fundamental library for scientific computing in Python. It provides support for efficient numerical operations and multi-dimensional array manipulation.

With NumPy, you can perform array operations, reshape arrays, and apply mathematical functions to arrays efficiently.

Pandas:

Pandas is a popular data manipulation library in Python. It provides high-performance data structures (such as DataFrame and Series) and data analysis tools.

Pandas allows you to load data from various file formats (CSV, Excel, SQL databases) and perform a wide range of data manipulation tasks, including filtering, sorting, grouping, merging, reshaping, and aggregating data.

Data Cleaning:

Python libraries like Pandas provide functions and methods for cleaning and preprocessing data.

You can handle missing data, remove duplicates, convert data types, handle outliers, and perform other data cleaning tasks to ensure the data is ready for analysis.

Data Transformation:

Python libraries offer various techniques to transform data. For example, you can apply mathematical functions, normalize or scale data, encode categorical variables, and create new derived features.

Pandas provides powerful methods for data transformation, such as applying functions to data, handling dates and time series, and working with text data.

Filtering and Querying:

Python libraries enable you to filter and query data based on specific conditions or criteria.

With Pandas, you can use boolean indexing, SQL-like query expressions, and logical operators to filter and select subsets of data that meet specific requirements.

Merging and Joining Data:

When working with multiple datasets, Python libraries like Pandas offer functions to merge or join datasets based on common columns or indices.

You can combine data from different sources, perform inner or outer joins, concatenate data along axes, and handle data alignment during merging.

Reshaping and Pivot Tables:

Python libraries provide functionality to reshape data and create pivot tables.

With Pandas, you can pivot, stack, or unstack data, transpose data, and reshape data between wide and long formats.

Handling Dates and Time Series:

Python libraries have features for working with dates, times, and time series data.

Libraries like Pandas provide tools to handle date and time data, perform date-based calculations, resample time series data, and generate time-based features.

These are just some of the essential techniques and libraries for data manipulation with Python. By leveraging these tools and techniques, you can efficiently process, transform, and manipulate data to extract valuable insights and support data-driven decision-making in various data science projects.

Data Visualization Basics

Data visualization is a powerful technique that allows you to represent data visually, making it easier to understand patterns, trends, and insights. Here are some basics of data visualization:

Choosing the Right Chart Type:

Selecting the appropriate chart type is crucial for effective data visualization. The choice depends on the nature of the data and the message you want to convey.

Common chart types include bar charts, line charts, scatter plots, pie charts, histograms, heatmaps, and more.

Consider factors such as the type of data (categorical, numerical, time series), the relationship between variables, and the intended audience when selecting the chart type.

Visual Encodings:

Visual encodings represent data using visual attributes such as position, length, angle, color, shape, and size.

Utilize appropriate encodings to accurately represent the data and facilitate comprehension. For example, use bar length for quantitative values, color for categorical variables, and position along an axis for time-related data.

Labels and Titles:

Clearly label the axes, data points, and any important features in your visualization.

Include a title that describes the purpose or main message of the visualization.

Labeling ensures that viewers can easily understand the data and interpret the visualization correctly.

Color Choice:

Choose colors carefully to enhance the clarity and aesthetics of your visualization.

Use color palettes that are visually appealing and provide good contrast between data categories or values.

Consider colorblind-friendly palettes to ensure accessibility for all viewers.

Data Scaling and Axis Limits:

Scale your data appropriately to prevent distortion or misrepresentation.

Set axis limits to focus on the relevant range of values and avoid misleading interpretations.

Adjust axis labels and ticks to provide meaningful intervals and make the data easier to interpret.

Annotations and Highlights:

Use annotations and highlights to draw attention to specific data points or interesting observations in your visualization.

Annotations can include text labels, arrows, or callouts that provide additional context or explanations.

Simplification and Emphasis:

Simplify complex visualizations by removing unnecessary clutter and simplifying the representation.

Emphasize key insights or trends by using visual cues like color, size, or positioning.

Iterative Design and Feedback:

Visualizations often require iteration and refinement. Seek feedback from others to improve the clarity and effectiveness of your visualization.

Test your visualization with different audiences to ensure it conveys the intended message and is understandable to a wide range of viewers.

Remember, the goal of data visualization is to effectively communicate insights and patterns in data. By following these basics, you can create clear and engaging visualizations that help your audience understand and derive value from the data.

Introduction to Machine Learning

Machine learning is a subfield of artificial intelligence (AI) that focuses on the development of algorithms and models that enable computers to learn from data and make predictions or decisions without being explicitly programmed. It involves the study of statistical and computational techniques that allow machines to automatically learn and improve from experience.

Here are some key concepts and components of machine learning:

Data:

Machine learning algorithms require data to learn patterns and make predictions.

Data can be structured (tabular data, databases) or unstructured (text, images, audio), and it serves as the input for training machine learning models.

Training Data and Labels:

In supervised learning, a training dataset is used to train the machine learning model.

The training dataset consists of input examples (features) and their corresponding known outputs (labels or target values).

The model learns patterns and relationships between the features and labels during the training process.

Algorithms and Models:

Machine learning algorithms are mathematical algorithms or computational procedures that analyze data, learn patterns, and make predictions or decisions.

Algorithms can be categorized into different types, such as regression, classification, clustering, and reinforcement learning, depending on the nature of the problem and the desired outcome.

These algorithms create machine learning models that encapsulate the learned patterns and relationships from the training data.

Training and Evaluation:

During the training phase, the machine learning model learns from the labeled training data by adjusting its internal parameters or weights.

The model tries to minimize the difference between its predicted outputs and the true labels in the training data.

After training, the model is evaluated using a separate validation or test dataset to assess its performance and generalization ability.

The evaluation metrics depend on the specific problem, such as accuracy, precision, recall, F1 score, or mean squared error.

Feature Engineering:

Feature engineering involves selecting, transforming, and creating relevant features from the raw data to improve the performance of the machine learning model.

It may involve techniques like normalization, scaling, one-hot encoding, dimensionality reduction, or creating new derived features.

Prediction and Inference:

Once trained, the machine learning model can make predictions or decisions on new, unseen data.

It takes the input features and applies the learned patterns to produce the desired output, such as predicting a class label or estimating a continuous value.

Unsupervised Learning:

In unsupervised learning, the machine learning algorithm explores and finds patterns in data without any labeled output.

It aims to discover hidden structures, clusters, or relationships within the data.

Deployment and Iterative Improvement:

Machine learning models are deployed in real-world applications to make predictions or decisions on new, incoming data.

Models can be continuously monitored and updated based on new data to improve their performance and adapt to changing conditions.

Machine learning finds applications in various domains, including image and speech recognition, natural language processing, recommendation systems, fraud detection, healthcare, finance, and more. It enables systems to automatically learn from data, improve over time, and make intelligent decisions without explicit programming.

Chapter 13: Introduction to Mobile App Development

Mobile App Development Platforms

Mobile app development platforms are software frameworks or environments that provide tools and resources for building mobile applications. These platforms simplify the app development process by offering pre-built components, libraries, and APIs that enable developers to create, test, and deploy apps more efficiently. Here are some popular mobile app development platforms:

Android Studio:

Android Studio is the official Integrated Development Environment (IDE) for Android app development.

It provides a comprehensive set of tools, including an Android emulator, code editor, debugger, and performance analyzer.

Android Studio supports Java and Kotlin programming languages and offers a wide range of libraries and APIs for building Android apps.

Xcode:

Xcode is the official IDE for iOS and macOS app development.

It offers a complete development environment with an interface builder, simulator, code editor, debugger, and performance analysis tools.

Xcode supports the Swift and Objective-C programming languages and provides access to the extensive iOS SDK (Software Development Kit) for building iOS, iPadOS, watchOS, and macOS apps.

React Native:

React Native is an open-source framework developed by Facebook for building cross-platform mobile apps.

It allows developers to write code once and deploy it on multiple platforms, such as Android and iOS.

React Native uses JavaScript and provides a bridge to native components, allowing for efficient app performance and native-like user experiences.

Flutter:

Flutter is a UI toolkit developed by Google for building natively compiled applications for mobile, web, and desktop platforms.

It uses the Dart programming language and offers a rich set of customizable UI widgets and libraries.

Flutter enables the development of visually appealing and high-performance apps with a single codebase that can be deployed on Android and iOS.

Xamarin:

Xamarin is a Microsoft-owned framework for building cross-platform mobile apps.

It allows developers to write code in C#, and the apps can be deployed on multiple platforms, including Android, iOS, and Windows.

Xamarin provides access to native APIs and platform-specific features, offering a native-like user experience.

PhoneGap/Cordova:

PhoneGap, also known as Apache Cordova, is an open-source framework for building mobile apps using web technologies such as HTML, CSS, and JavaScript.

It enables developers to create hybrid apps that run within a WebView, providing access to native device features through JavaScript APIs.

PhoneGap/Cordova supports multiple platforms, including Android, iOS, Windows Phone, and more.

Appcelerator Titanium:

Appcelerator Titanium is a cross-platform development platform that allows developers to build native mobile apps using JavaScript.

It provides access to native APIs and features through JavaScript code and supports various platforms, including Android and iOS.

Appcelerator Titanium offers a comprehensive set of development tools and resources for efficient app development.

These platforms offer different approaches to mobile app development, catering to various programming languages, frameworks, and development preferences. The choice of platform depends on factors such as target platforms, development resources, project requirements, and developer expertise.

Native vs. Cross-Platform Development

Native development and cross-platform development are two approaches to building mobile applications, each with its own advantages and considerations. Here's a comparison between the two:

Native Development:

Native development involves building mobile apps specifically for a single platform, such as Android or iOS.

It uses platform-specific programming languages (Java or Kotlin for Android, Swift or Objective-C for iOS) and development tools (Android Studio for Android, Xcode for iOS).

Native apps have access to the full range of platform-specific features and APIs, providing high performance and seamless integration with the operating system.

They can take full advantage of the device's hardware capabilities, providing smooth user experiences and better performance.

Native development allows for deep customization and adherence to platform-specific design guidelines, resulting in apps that feel native to the platform.

However, native development requires separate codebases for different platforms, which can result in increased development time and effort.

Maintenance and updates may also require separate implementations for each platform.

Cross-Platform Development:

Cross-platform development allows for building mobile apps that can run on multiple platforms, such as Android and iOS, using a single codebase.

It typically uses frameworks like React Native, Flutter, Xamarin, or PhoneGap/Cordova, which provide abstraction layers and allow developers to write code once and deploy it across platforms.

Cross-platform frameworks often use web technologies like HTML, CSS, and JavaScript or specialized languages like Dart or C#.

With cross-platform development, development time and effort are reduced since a single codebase can be used for multiple platforms.

Changes and updates can be applied to all platforms simultaneously, streamlining the maintenance process.

However, cross-platform apps may not have access to the full range of platform-specific features and APIs, and performance may be slightly lower compared to native apps.

User interfaces may require additional effort to ensure they adhere to platform-specific design guidelines and provide a native-like experience.

Factors to Consider:

Development Time and Cost: Cross-platform development generally reduces development time and cost by sharing code across platforms. Native development may require more effort and resources due to separate codebases.

Performance and User Experience: Native apps generally provide better performance and seamless user experiences as they leverage platform-specific capabilities. Cross-platform apps may have slightly lower performance and may require additional effort to achieve a native-like experience.

Access to Platform-Specific Features: Native development offers full access to platform-specific features and APIs. Cross-platform frameworks provide varying levels of access to these features, and some may require additional configuration or customization.

Developer Skill Set: Consider the skills and expertise of your development team. Native development requires knowledge of platform-specific languages and tools, while cross-platform development may rely on web technologies or specialized languages.

Ultimately, the choice between native and cross-platform development depends on factors such as project requirements, time-to-market considerations, budget constraints, target audience, and the trade-offs you are willing to make in terms of performance, customization, and development effort.

Building a Simple Mobile App

Building a simple mobile app involves several steps, from conceptualizing the idea to deploying the app on a device. Here is a high-level overview of the process:

Define the App Idea:

Begin by defining the purpose and functionality of your app. Identify the problem it will solve or the value it will provide to users.

Plan the App Structure and Flow:

Determine the screens, features, and navigation flow of your app. Sketch out a wireframe or create a storyboard to visualize the user interface and interactions.

Choose the Development Approach:

Decide whether you want to develop a native app for a specific platform (Android or iOS) or opt for cross-platform development using frameworks like React Native or Flutter.

Consider factors such as target audience, development resources, time constraints, and desired platform-specific features.

Set Up the Development Environment:

Install the necessary development tools and SDKs based on your chosen platform and development approach.

For native development, set up Android Studio (for Android) or Xcode (for iOS). For cross-platform development, install the relevant framework and associated tools.

Develop the App's UI and Features:

Start implementing the user interface (UI) of your app, following the planned structure and flow.

Use platform-specific UI components or cross-platform UI widgets provided by the chosen framework.

Implement the required features and functionality based on the app's requirements, such as user authentication, data input, or integration with APIs.

Test and Debug:

Regularly test your app during development to identify and fix any bugs or issues.

Test the app's functionality, UI responsiveness, and compatibility across different devices and screen sizes.

Utilize debugging tools and techniques to diagnose and resolve any issues that arise.

Refine the App's Design:

Polish the app's UI design, ensuring it is visually appealing, intuitive, and user-friendly.

Incorporate user feedback and iterate on the design to improve the overall user experience.

Perform User Acceptance Testing:

Involve potential users or beta testers to evaluate the app's usability and provide feedback.

Incorporate user feedback to further refine and enhance the app's functionality and user experience.

Prepare for Deployment:

Create developer accounts on relevant app stores (Google Play Store, Apple App Store) if you plan to distribute the app publicly.

Follow the guidelines and requirements set by the app stores, including app metadata, icons, screenshots, and privacy policies.

Deploy and Publish:

Build the app for the target platform and prepare it for distribution.

Submit the app to the respective app stores for review and approval.

Once approved, the app will be available for users to download and use.

Monitor, Update, and Maintain:

Monitor user feedback and app performance after deployment.

Continuously update and maintain the app to address issues, add new features, and improve user satisfaction.

Remember, building a mobile app requires both technical skills and creativity. Take the time to plan, design, and test your app thoroughly to ensure a positive user experience.

Chapter 14: Final Project and Beyond

Selecting a Project Idea

Selecting a project idea for your mobile app can be an exciting but challenging task. Here are some tips to help you choose a compelling and feasible project idea:

Identify a Problem or Need:

Look for problems or needs in your own life or within a particular industry or community.

Consider areas where technology can provide solutions or improve existing processes.

Research Market Demand:

Conduct market research to understand the demand for similar apps or solutions.

Look for gaps or areas that are underserved or have room for innovation.

Define Your Target Audience:

Clearly define the target audience for your app.

Consider their demographics, interests, preferences, and pain points.

Tailor your app idea to address their specific needs and provide value.

Evaluate Feasibility and Complexity:

Assess the feasibility of implementing your app idea, considering technical requirements, available resources, and time constraints.

Start with a project scope that is manageable and achievable within your resources.

Brainstorm and Refine Ideas:

Generate multiple app ideas through brainstorming sessions.

Evaluate each idea based on its uniqueness, potential impact, and alignment with your skills and interests.

Refine and narrow down your ideas to choose the most promising one.

Consider Monetization Potential:

Think about how your app can generate revenue.

Explore different monetization models such as in-app purchases, subscriptions, advertising, or partnerships.

Validate the Idea:

Validate your app idea by seeking feedback from potential users or experts in the industry.

Conduct surveys, interviews, or focus groups to gather insights and validate the demand for your app.

Assess Technical Requirements:

Consider the technical requirements and skills needed to implement your app idea.

Evaluate if you have the necessary expertise or if you can acquire the skills required.

Align with Your Interests and Expertise:

Choose an idea that aligns with your interests, expertise, and long-term goals.

Passion for the project will keep you motivated during the development process.

Balance Innovation and Execution:

Aim for a balance between innovative ideas and practicality.

While it's important to offer unique features, ensure that your app idea is viable and has a clear value proposition.

Remember, the best app ideas often come from understanding user needs and providing solutions that add value to their lives. Take the time to research, validate, and refine your ideas before committing to a specific project.

Planning and Designing Your Project

Planning and designing your project is a critical phase in the development process. It helps establish a clear vision, outline the project scope, and define the key elements of your mobile app. Here are some steps to consider when planning and designing your project:

Define Project Goals and Objectives:

Clearly define the goals and objectives of your project. What problem will your app solve? What specific outcomes do you want to achieve?

Identify Target Audience:

Identify and understand your target audience. Define their demographics, needs, and preferences. This will help shape the design and functionality of your app.

Create User Personas:

Develop user personas, fictional representations of your target users, to gain insights into their behaviors, motivations, and goals. This will aid in designing a user-centered app.

Conduct Market Research:

Research your competitors and analyze existing apps in your target market. Identify their strengths, weaknesses, and opportunities to differentiate your app.

Outline App Features and Functionality:

List the core features and functionality your app will offer. Prioritize them based on user needs and their importance to achieving your project goals.

Create a Wireframe or Prototype:

Develop a visual representation of your app's layout and functionality using wireframing or prototyping tools. This will help you visualize the app's flow and structure.

Design User Interface (UI) and User Experience (UX):

Design a visually appealing and intuitive UI that aligns with your target audience and your app's brand.

Focus on providing a seamless and engaging user experience, ensuring easy navigation, clear actions, and informative feedback.

Develop a Technical Architecture:

Define the technical architecture of your app, including the choice of programming languages, frameworks, and third-party libraries.

Plan the data storage, server requirements, APIs, and any integrations needed for your app's functionality.

Plan Iterative Development:

Break down your project into smaller milestones or sprints to facilitate an iterative development process.

Prioritize features and functionalities for each iteration, ensuring regular feedback and testing throughout the development cycle.

Create a Project Timeline:

Create a timeline that outlines the major milestones, tasks, and deadlines for your project. This will help track progress and ensure timely delivery.

Consider Security and Privacy:

Incorporate security measures to protect user data and ensure the privacy of your app's users.

Plan for authentication, encryption, and secure data transmission as necessary.

Test and QA Strategy:

Define a testing and quality assurance (QA) strategy to ensure a bug-free and stable app.

Determine the testing methodologies, tools, and resources needed for thorough testing.

Define Metrics and Analytics:

Determine the metrics and analytics you will track to measure the success of your app. This can include user engagement, retention rates, conversion rates, and other key performance indicators (KPIs).

Establish a Budget:

Consider the financial resources required for developing, launching, and maintaining your app. Define a budget to ensure proper allocation of resources throughout the project.

Collaboration and Communication:

Establish effective communication channels and collaboration tools to facilitate smooth coordination among team members and stakeholders.

Planning and designing your project provides a roadmap for successful app development. It helps align the team, set expectations, and ensure that your app meets user needs and achieves its intended goals. Regularly review and refine your plans as the project progresses to adapt to evolving requirements and feedback.

Implementing Your Project

Implementing your project involves the actual development and coding of your mobile app. Here are some key steps to consider during the implementation phase:

Set Up the Development Environment:

Install the necessary software development tools and frameworks based on your chosen platform and technology stack.

Ensure that you have a working development environment with all the required dependencies.

Break Down the Project into Tasks:

Divide your project into smaller, manageable tasks based on the features and functionality defined during the planning phase.

Create a task list or use project management tools to track progress and assign tasks to team members.

Start with the Core Functionality:

Begin by implementing the core functionality of your app. Focus on the essential features that align with your project goals and user needs.

Prioritize the implementation of these features to ensure a functional base for your app.

Follow Coding Best Practices:

Adhere to coding best practices and industry standards.

Write clean, modular, and well-documented code that is easy to understand, maintain, and scale.

Use meaningful variable and function names, follow consistent coding style conventions, and leverage code comments to explain complex logic.

Implement User Interface (UI) and User Experience (UX):

Translate the wireframes or prototypes created during the design phase into actual UI components and layouts.

Pay attention to usability, responsiveness, and accessibility.

Ensure that the UI elements align with the defined user experience and design guidelines.

Integrate Backend Services:

If your app requires backend services, integrate them into your app's architecture.

Implement server-side logic, APIs, database connections, and any necessary integrations with external services.

Ensure secure handling of user data and proper validation of inputs.

Test and Debug:

Conduct thorough testing to identify and fix any bugs or issues in your app.

Perform unit testing, integration testing, and user acceptance testing to ensure the app functions as intended.

Utilize debugging tools and techniques to identify and resolve any runtime errors or logical issues.

Optimize Performance:

Optimize your app's performance to ensure smooth operation and responsiveness.

Consider factors such as memory usage, network requests, and rendering efficiency.

Analyze and optimize code snippets or algorithms that may impact performance.

Implement Error Handling and Exceptional Cases:

Implement error handling mechanisms to gracefully handle unexpected scenarios and exceptions.

Validate user inputs and handle edge cases to prevent crashes or undesired behavior.

Incorporate Analytics and Tracking:

Integrate analytics and tracking tools to gather data on user behavior, usage patterns, and app performance.

Collect relevant metrics and key performance indicators (KPIs) to measure the success of your app.

Regularly Review and Refactor Code:

Continuously review and refactor your codebase to improve readability, maintainability, and performance.

Identify areas for optimization or code reuse.

Consider code reviews and conduct periodic code refactoring to ensure code quality.

Documentation:

Document your code, APIs, and any relevant information that can assist with future maintenance or further development.

Include instructions for setting up the development environment and any dependencies.

Version Control and Collaboration:

Use version control systems (e.g., Git) to track changes, collaborate with team members, and manage codebase history.

Follow branching and merging best practices to ensure a smooth development workflow.

Iterative Development:

Adopt an iterative development approach, releasing incremental updates and incorporating user feedback.

Continuously improve your app based on user feedback, bug reports, and performance metrics.

Prepare for Deployment:

Prepare your app for deployment by optimizing its size, resources, and dependencies.

- Perform final testing on various devices and platforms to ensure compatibility and stability.

Remember, implementing your project requires a structured and organized approach. Regular communication and collaboration among team members, along with continuous testing and quality assurance, will help ensure the successful implementation of your mobile app.

Testing and Refining Your Project

Testing and refining your project is a crucial phase in the development process. It involves evaluating the functionality, performance, and user experience of your mobile app to identify and address any issues or areas for improvement. Here are some steps to consider during the testing and refinement phase:

Test Plan Creation:

Develop a comprehensive test plan that outlines the testing objectives, test cases, and testing methodologies to be used.

Identify the different types of testing, such as functional testing, usability testing, performance testing, and security testing.

Functional Testing:

Conduct functional testing to verify that your app meets the specified requirements and performs its intended functions.

Test each feature and interaction to ensure they work as expected and produce the desired outcomes.

Usability Testing:

Evaluate the usability of your app by testing it with representative users.

Gather feedback on the app's ease of use, navigation, and overall user experience.

Incorporate user feedback to refine the app's design and optimize the user interface.

Performance Testing:

Assess the performance of your app under different scenarios and workloads.

Measure factors such as response times, loading speeds, and resource usage.

Identify and resolve any bottlenecks or performance issues that may impact the user experience.

Compatibility Testing:

Test your app on various devices, screen sizes, and operating system versions to ensure compatibility and consistent behavior across different platforms.

Address any layout issues, scaling problems, or device-specific challenges.

Security Testing:

Conduct security testing to identify vulnerabilities and protect user data.

Test for common security risks such as unauthorized access, data breaches, and injection attacks.

Implement encryption, authentication mechanisms, and secure coding practices to safeguard user information.

Error Handling and Exception Testing:

Evaluate how your app handles errors, exceptions, and edge cases.

Test scenarios where unexpected inputs or situations occur, and ensure that the app gracefully handles errors without crashing or compromising data integrity.

Beta Testing:

Engage beta testers or a small group of users to test your app in real-world conditions.

Collect feedback on usability, functionality, and performance to identify areas for improvement.

Address reported issues and incorporate user suggestions to enhance the app's quality.

Continuous Integration and Regression Testing:

Implement a continuous integration and delivery (CI/CD) pipeline to automate the testing and deployment process.

Conduct regression testing after each code change or update to ensure that existing features continue to work as expected.

Analyze User Feedback and Metrics:

Collect and analyze user feedback, reviews, and app usage metrics to gain insights into user satisfaction and identify areas for further improvement.

Use app analytics tools to track user engagement, retention rates, and conversion rates to assess the app's performance.

Iterative Refinement:

Based on the test results, user feedback, and performance metrics, make iterative improvements to your app.

Address reported bugs, fix issues, optimize performance, and enhance the user experience in subsequent app updates.

Documentation and Knowledge Sharing:

Maintain updated documentation that includes known issues, resolutions, and testing procedures.

Share lessons learned and insights gained from the testing process with the development team to improve future projects.

Remember, testing is an ongoing process, and refining your app based on feedback and insights is crucial for ensuring its quality and success. Continuously iterate, gather user feedback, and make improvements to deliver a polished and user-friendly mobile app.

Conclusion

Congratulations on completing this immersive journey into the world of programming! You've come a long way, starting from the basics of programming and gradually building a strong foundation in various programming languages, data manipulation, web development, and even mobile app development.

Throughout this book, you've learned the essential concepts and techniques that form the bedrock of software development. You've grasped the power of problem-solving, logical thinking, and algorithmic design. You've become familiar with different programming languages and gained the ability to choose the right tool for the job. You've explored data structures, object-oriented programming, and the principles of good software design. And you've acquired the skills to test, debug, and refine your code to ensure its quality and reliability.

But remember, this is just the beginning of your programming journey. The field of programming is constantly evolving, with new technologies, languages, and frameworks emerging every day. Embrace the mindset of continuous learning and stay curious. Seek out new challenges, tackle complex problems, and never be afraid to dive into uncharted territories.

As you continue your programming endeavors, remember the importance of collaboration and community. Engage with other developers, share your knowledge, and contribute to the open-source community. The power of collective wisdom and collaboration can take your skills and projects to new heights.

Always strive for excellence in your code. Write clean, well-documented, and maintainable code that others can understand and build upon. Embrace best practices, keep up with industry standards, and be open to adopting new technologies and methodologies.

Lastly, never forget the impact you can make with your programming skills. Whether it's creating innovative software solutions, improving efficiency in existing systems, or contributing to meaningful projects, you have the potential to make a difference in the world through your code.

So, go forth with confidence, armed with the knowledge and skills you've gained from this book. Embrace the challenges, explore your passions, and unleash your creativity through programming. The possibilities are limitless, and the future is yours to shape.

Thank you for joining us on this incredible journey into the realm of programming. We hope this book has inspired you, motivated you, and provided you with a solid foundation to embark on your own coding adventures.

Happy coding, and may your programming endeavors be filled with excitement, growth, and endless opportunities!

9 781803 425566